Self Creation

John,
Dreams do Come
True go for them!

Yvonne Brown

Self Creation

10 Powerful Principles For Changing Your Life

Yvonne F. Brown

ISBN 0-9724318-0-2

Library of Congress Cataloging-in-Publication Data

Self Help, Business, Motivation, Life Skills, Success

Published by JAD Publications a division of Ball of Gold Corporation

ATTENTION SCHOOLS AND CORPORATIONS:
Self Creation is available at quantity discounts with bulk purchase for educational, business or sales promotional use. For information please write to: **SPECIAL SALES DEPARTMENT, JAD PUBLICATIONS, P.O. Box 577405, Chicago, IL 60657-7405 U.S.A.**

This book was printed in the United States of America.

Contents

Friends like me

Friends like me are born to be,
Forever loving subtly,
To cherish your endearing heart,
And fear the times we are apart,
Foreboding that still other love,
Of sea, of earth, the sky above,
Those things that make us love the new,
And wanting still to be with you

© William L. Brown, July 11th, 1998

DEDICATION

To my grandmother Gong Gong
Who told me I could do whatever I put my mind to
I think of you everyday and
I miss you

To my husband Bill
Who reminds me how special I am everyday
This book would not be possible
Without your help and support
I love you!

To my son Charles
You are the light of my life
I am so proud of you and
I thank you for your support
Always remember that I love you

Here's what people say about *Self Creation—10 Powerful Principles For Changing Your Life* by Yvonne F. Brown . . .

"Can the heart write? Can the mind feel? Yvonne Brown has put mind and heart into every page of *Self Creation*. In a style that speaks from her heart and makes you feel as if you 're listening to your best friend (and you may be), she opens your mind to the exciting possibility of Self Creation. Each chapter is woven with powerful stories that take you by the heart. Yvonne then takes you by the mind with irrefutable logic as you follow the steps that will lead you to becoming the person you've always known you could be. You owe it to yourself to create that person with the help of Yvonne Brown's *Self Creation*"

Michael Wynne, president,
International Management Consulting Associates
and past president, National Speakers Association.

"This Jamaican American dreamer has written a book that will help awaken your dreams and will provide the templates and guidance to make those dreams come true. It's time to stop procrastinating about your dreams; it 's time to buy this book."

Rita Emmett, author of *The Procrastinator's Handbook* and
The Procrastinating Child: A Handbook for
Adults to Help Children Stop Putting Things Off.

"This fast-moving practical book is full of wisdom and insights for living a better, fuller life."

Brian Tracy, Author of Victory!

"Yvonne has given us an interesting and insightful look at how to change our life story and outcomes, filled with numerous personal examples that most of us can relate to. An easy yet thought-provoking read that will challenge and motivate you."

Tim Connor, Certified Speaking Professional
and best selling author/speaker/trainer.

"The principles in this book provide the guidance needed to identify your strengths, energize your life, and take control of your future. Yvonne Brown has written a book that will help you to take control of your destiny. Read it, then re-read it and learn how you can live the life you've always imagined."

Willie Jolley, author of It Only Takes A Minute To Change YourLife and A Setback Is A Setup For A Comeback!

"This book is a book that you will want to read over and over again. Every time you pick up this book and read the insights, you will view your life differently and positively. Practical anecdotes and pure wisdom that will help you create your best life!"

Robert Pino, Life Alchemist and author of Absolute Victory.

Foreword

Once upon a time on a tiny little island called Jamaica a little girl named Yvonne looked up at a theatre screen and dreamed. She dreamed of a life of abundance filled with the opportunities and beauty that she saw in the movies. When she thumbed through magazines and read her books she dreamed of traveling to far away exotic places with marble floors. "One day," she softly told herself, "I will walk those streets and sleep in beds with canopies." She never told a soul but made herself a promise that the dream would come true.

This Jamaican American Dreamer soon came to America and set about achievement of those dreams. What happens when you set goals, create a plan for the future and work the plan? What if the universe is abundant and limitless and eager to help you to achieve your dreams? Upon arriving in the United States she set about fulfillment of her dreams and over a period of time eventually achieved them.

She decided to become a fashion model and was able to not only achieve it, but was successful at it. Then she decided to become a singer and eventually achieved that too. There were certain strategies that she soon found were repeatable and always worked for achievement of her dreams. Making note of them she used them to change careers again and again often re-creating herself into the image she saw in her mind's eye. Then one day she realized that these strategies would work for anyone and decided to put pen to paper and share them so that everyone could use them for their own self-creation. This is that book.

There are two types of people in this world, those who talk about doing something and those who actually execute on their ideas. In order to be successful you must be one of those who execute. You can talk about doing something for years but if you don't execute its all for naught. If you want to be happy and successful you must take charge of your life and your future, and the way to do that is through self-creation.

Success today can be measured in many ways. For some it is financial freedom, for others, it is a stress-free life, some people measure success by the freedom to execute on an idea and run their own company as an entrepreneur. However you choose to define it, the key is that you define what success means to you.

Since September 11, 2001 many American citizens have begun examining what success means to them. Many people have changed their careers and returned to a 'simpler' life. In any event now more than ever, we define what we want our future to be and that future is often self-shaped.

This book will help you on your way to creating the life you always wanted. It will show you through stories and an example how sometimes the thing that seems to be a setback is actually the best thing that ever happened to you and really sets you up for getting to the next level and perhaps your greatest achievement. I encourage you to read it and use the principles contained here to accelerate yourself to the life you always dreamed possible.

—Les Brown

Chapter 1

Principle One

Check Your Premise

Man's unique reward, however, is that while animals survive by adjusting themselves to their background, man survives by adjusting his background to himself.

Ayn Rand

Chapter 1

Check Your Premise

What are your guiding principles? On what foundation is your idea of yourself based?

If you've found this book, the chances are excellent that you have reached yet another crossroad in your life and are, yourself, a seeker. What guidance can be had, then, before taking your next steps? This curiosity of ours, this seeking, means that we are thoughtful persons who do not make important choices lightly.

It is this author's premise, that in writing this book and sharing my own experiences and thoughts, that your pot of thoughts will be stirred in ways that I can only imagine. So let us endeavor together, by fearlessly looking at what brought you and I to this point.

What is your history?

Our personal history has a direct bearing on our mindset and how we react to events in our lives. It also impacts our perceptions of events and our response to them. Often, our situation is "cast"—that which we are born into. This is always an obstacle to understanding how others feel about the exact same events, their perceptions and oh so different responses.

What is a mindset? Webster defines "mindset" as a "fixed mental attitude formed by experience, education, prejudice, etc." And our mindset is exactly the reason why we are predisposed to perceive and respond to events as we do. Therefore, examining our own personal history is fundamental to gaining insight into how and why we regard and perceive specific events so differently.

Before we can make sense of it all, we need to examine our own personal historical background. That's right, make it personal. The life issues and events that matter most to us as individuals must be observed within a framework that helps us to understand their significance to us. Why is that so important to you? Well. If you've ever been asked the question—check your premise. It's probably valid, but maybe it's not. Maybe it's a product of your history.

Knowing our own personal history, and how it is remembered, can help us to distinguish rationale from the foundation of our core beliefs. A youngster who was raised to believe that "you're stupid" most likely internalizes this statement and proceeds through life fulfilling this prophecy. Without realizing that this is a false and inaccurate perception of who they are, this child has a major hurdle to overcome.

In perceiving the world, and what happens in our lives, we tend to think that we are in charge of what's input to our thinking. But sometimes the wiring in our internal computer is surrogate-programmed as input that pleases, leaving how it is to be offered to an outsider, and how it is to be processed to you. It takes considerable effort to change our habitual way of perceiving and reasoning and to break out of our established mindsets. Thus, our conscious selves, left untended, are not so much in charge as we think.

You are the sum of your experiences and your self-control. Your self-esteem and how you perceive events must be driven from the inside out. The good news is . . . even if you have been subject to low self-esteem, or even no self-esteem, you can make the decision to do something about it and recreate yourself to be a self-actualized being. You can begin today to build your self-esteem and empower your own self-creation. Our first step is to face our self and to look at our history. Then identify the principles which shall be yours. It's about you, and determines what steps you will take to create your future. Let's call this your personal "manifest destiny".

Jamaica, British West Indies

I was born in Kingston, Jamaica before the West Indies won independence from Britain. I went to Catholic schools starting in kindergarten where I attended Saint Anne's primary school. I led a very sheltered childhood and was very active in the church choir. After winning a scholarship, I attended Immaculate Conception High School, an all girl school and convent where I spent my high school years surrounded by nuns.

My mother immigrated to the United States when I was only 3-months old and left me with my grandparents. My dad left for America when my brother was one year old and my mother was carrying me. I was to have left for America with her but my mother's visa came when I was three months old and since I did not have a visa, I could not accompany her.

My dad immigrated to America to attend college for his degree in Electrical Engineering, and in search of a better life for himself and his family. The plan was to send for my brother and me within the year; the reality was that I did not receive my visa until 17 years later. Frankly, each year my parents had another child (for a total of eight more children) and the funds that should have brought Donnie and I to the United States was instead used for medical expenses. I did not know it at the time, but this was a blessing in disguise.

Growing up on the island, we did not have television or even a telephone and in my opinion we didn't need them, as there was so much to do anyway. We did have the radio though, and so were not completely cut off from the world. I loved books; and reading became my means of travel to exotic places and to learning and self-growth. Some of my favorite books were, The Fountainhead and Atlas Shrugged by Ayn Rand, Brave New World, by Aldous Huxley and since I was an English Lit major, many of the works of William Shakespeare.

We had the Tivoli movie theatre for entertainment and, along with Ayn Rand, Aldous Huxley and Shakespeare I could dream and learn about the possibilities for my future.

My grandparents were strong, proud people and taught me that I could do anything I set my mind to. They told me that I was smart and that if I ever wanted to do anything in life, I should 'go for it' because there is nothing worse in life than sitting at the end of the journey saying "I coulda, I woulda, I shoulda," That, they told me, is truly a waste of life. They also told me, "some things can only be accomplished while you are young, so go for them while you can. If you fail, it doesn't matter, for at least you will have tried."

This philosophy is part of my mindset to this day and my typical approach to life and its difficulties. I tend to take the leap of faith and trust in the universe, and I encourage you to do the same.

Baba

My grandfather was called Baba because he was one a barber and owned several barber shops. Baba, was a self made man. He was orphaned at a very early age, yet through daring, found a way to travel from Jamaica to Nicaragua and experience lifestyles and cultures outside of the island. He became an entrepreneur, owning several barbershops all over the island, and had several employees in each shop working for him.

Baba was a total character, seen riding a motorcycle around the island from barbershop to barbershop picking up his daily revenue, in cash, with a pistol on his hip. He did this even when he was in his sixties, so I can just imagine how wild he must have been as a young man in those decades before I was born

He never learned how to read or write, and like most illiterate business people, found ways to keep it hidden from his employees and business partners. Nevertheless, baba ruled his domain.

The Routine at Kingston

Early each morning Baba would get all of the newspapers in town and we [his grandchildren] would read each newspaper to him from cover to cover. You see we could read because Baba was fanatical about his children and grandchildren having an education. In fact he paid for extra classes after school to ensure we would succeed.

His retention of the events and news of the day was such that he could converse with anyone about any news item of the day as though he had read it himself. Thus no one ever learned that he could not read. This, by the way, is a common trait among the illiterate.

Most news on the Island was by word of mouth or from the local (and only) newspaper, The Daily Gleaner

Baba wore a 45 like a clothing item, when he picked up the daily receipts from his numerous barbershops, and everyone knew he was a pretty tough character Suffice it say, he was never bothered by robbers. As a little girl, I once picked up his deadly weapon, and the sheer weight of the thing nearly felled me.

Every Sunday I would take all of the money from the week's earnings and put it on top of the kitchen table. I would separate the different types of coins and bills and stack them in piles then count them. Baba would then separate each man's wages for the week and set it aside in an envelope to pay them on Monday morning. In those days, Jamaica did not have an income tax so this made payroll a fairly straightforward and simple task. Value for value.

Baba had a collection of little tin cans, one for each of his grandchildren and labeled with their name. After the payroll and other financial tasks were complete, he would dispense an equal sum of money in each and put it away for special occasions. When birthdays and Christmas rolled around, Baba would open each child's little tin can and use what money he found there to purchase the birthday or Christmas gift that was that child's desire.

As I recall, we always got our heart's desire. If it was a bike or hula-hoop or pretty doll, whatever it was, we got what we wanted. If the tin can did not have enough to purchase the prized object, Baba would just add the needed funds to ensure that each grandchild received what they wished for.

Oh, and by the way, if you got good grades in school or attained some achievement, he would add something extra to your tin can as an *additional reward and incentive* for future accomplishments.

Baba had a big thing about education. It was very important to him, perhaps it is because he did not have a formal education himself, but like any parent he wanted the best for his children. Whatever the reason, he paid for us to take extra classes and study for exams hoping we'd qualify for a scholarship to a private school.

The investment paid off, and when I was 12 years old, I won a scholarship to Immaculate Conception High School in Constant Springs. My siblings won scholarships, too, and we were all so proud of ourselves; it was great!

The scholarship program worked is like this: all of the children who had taken these extra classes were eligible to take the scholarship tests and, if you passed, your name was published in the newspaper. I remember how we kids couldn't wait to get the paper the morning the results were published, to look for our names. This was a big event with parents and children alike waiting for the paper and jostling to be the first to find out who had won a scholarship that year.

One special aspect of the program at that time is that the exam papers were sent to England to be graded, thus ensuring an impartial evaluation of each child's ability. The educators who graded the papers never knew who the students were so you were awarded the scholarship based on your own merit and ability.

Depending on the final grades, the winners had the option of attending the high school of their choice or a technical school. I won a scholarship for either Alpha Academy or Immaculate Conception High School. I chose Immaculate Conception High School, remembering that all the *bad* girls went to Alpha Academy. And besides, Immaculate was regarded as the best school on the island, so the choice was an obvious one for me.

The nice thing about winning such a scholarship is that not only the school tuition was paid in full, but school uniforms and schoolbooks were paid for as well with the scholarship funds. I don't recall who provided the funds, only that I was fortunate enough to have won the scholarship to one of the most prestigious high schools on the island. Your parents only need pay for your bus fare and encourage your academic success. All *you* had to do is study hard and do well in school.

Immaculate Conception

Immaculate Conception is an all girls Catholic High School in Constant Springs, Jamaica. Its campus resides on an incredibly beautiful estate that was given to the Catholic Church by a wealthy patron.

The bus ride from Kingston is a very long one, and we pass several all boys high schools, and Alpha Academy, before arriving at Immaculate. There are monitors aboard the school bus to ensure decorum is preserved and that the proper good girls riding *do not* succumb to the temptation to talk to boys. It was strictly against the rules for Immaculate Conception girls to talk to boys while wearing their school uniform. This was a big deal and sternly enforced.

The Immaculate Conception High School uniform is comprised of a white pleated skirt, white short sleeve blouse (neatly tucked in), navy blue necktie, preferably with a Windsor knot. The shoes are brown penny loafers (if you could get an American penny to put in it you were *extra* special) and brown anklet socks, meaning that the socks are folded down twice so that they never reach higher than your ankle.

The topper is a wide-brimmed straw hat with a brown ribbon tied in a bow at the back, the ends streaming down the center of the wearers back. No flamboyant hairdos are permitted; the hat must sit flat on the head.

Above all, no sleeveless blouses or patent leather shoes were to be tolerated. Sleeveless blouses might afford the boys an occasion to see your breast {totally unacceptable} and as we all know, patent leather shoes reflect one's panties. Such loose morals may have been acceptable over at Alpha Academy, but Immaculate Conception isn't called that for nothing.

The gate to Immaculate has a high semi-circular metal sign with the name "Immaculate Conception High School" punched into it beyond which you'll travel about another half a mile before reaching the first buildings. This is the senior part of the school and is separated from the newer buildings by an oval shaped garden containing apple trees and lots of sectioned off areas in which a variety of flowers bloom with abandon. There are benches within each of these sections of flowers that seem to invite you to reflect on life, relax or do homework, and often several nuns can be seen walking the paths as they say their rosaries.

Turning left, you can see the convent where the nuns live and the boarding school where the mostly European foreigner students reside. Just beyond these buildings is the junior high school. Continuing along the path, you arrive at the large gazebo where school plays are held in the open area, and where students' gym and fencing classes take place. Left of this is an outdoor Olympic-size swimming pool and the grassy area where softball and cricket are played.

There is a chapel around to the right and my favorite item in this area was the "dog castle". This particular feature might require further explanation should the Queen ever have visited. It was nothing less than a replica of an English castle, built for use as the doghouse. I can remember how much I enjoyed watching the dogs stick their heads out of the different windows of the castle. It was a fun game to play with them.

The entire school is surrounded by a golf course, also owned by the Catholic Church. The backdrop and surroundings of all this is the Blue Mountain Peaks. Needless to say, the marvelous estate is very picturesque, and quite conducive to study.

I was required to do 3 hours of homework every night whether I had homework or not. "If you don't have any homework, then read ahead," Baba would say. "That way, you will be ready when the teacher talks about the next part of the subject during class." I don't know for sure, but I think that because he couldn't read, Baba had a great deal of respect for education and always encouraged us to go on to college and "get that degree."

I regret that he had passed away before he was able to see me walk across the stage to accept my Bachelor of Arts degree. I know it would have made him proud.

Gang-Gang

My grandmother, Gang-Gang, was an imposing woman of over six feet in height, with a formidable presence to match. She was part Arawak Indian and a true Jamaican. She could ride a horse bareback and swim with the current in a natural whirlpool. Her parents died when she was about 14 years old. She and Baba became a couple in their teens and though they married others later were close for their entire life. My mother was their only child.

Gang-Gang was also an entrepreneur who owned a bar in the days when women did not own their own businesses. In fact, in those days American women were not even allowed to vote, to have their own credit, or get patents for their inventions. Gang-Gang not only owned her own bar, but *she was the bouncer.* She could whip any man there in a fair fight, and though good-natured, took no guff from anybody.

Despite her innate toughness, Gang-Gang was a real fashion plate. I mean she really loved to dress up. She would often wear a pretty dress, matching shoes, big floppy hat and white gloves. The whole dressing up bit became a tradition that I still carry on today. I love floppy hats—and have many—and while white gloves have gone out of style, I still love to dress up too. Gang-Gang was strong willed, beautiful and smart, and I miss her very much.

Believe in yourself and the strength of your convictions

Gang-Gang had diabetes and would give herself insulin every day. Once she got a cut on her hand that would not heal. When she went to the hospital, they admitted her and then informed her that they would have to amputate her hand because it would not heal. Looking at the medical options available, the physicians truly believed that amputation of the hand was her only real choice.

I remember how she said, "Get my clothes, Yvonne. We're going home!" Then she turned to the doctor, held up her hand, and said, "You see this hand? When I go to my grave, it will still be attached."

After we returned home, Gang-Gang went into the backyard and pulled some herbs from the ground. She rubbed the herbs together in her hands until they were moist, then she packed the herbs on her swollen hand and bandaged it up. After many such self-administered treatments, Gang Gang's hand healed completely.

She then returned to the hospital, found her doctor and showed him her healed hand. "See? I told you I would be able to keep my hand," she said. Then she wiggled her fingers and showed him that they worked as well. The stunned doctor had many questions for her and they launched into a deep discussion about her herbal treatment. After she explained to him what treatment she had used, we went home.

I'll never forget how, with the courage of her convictions, her strong will, and with sheer determination, my grandmother showed the doctor that there are many different types of treatments and remedies for an ailment.

This was just one of the great lessons that I got from Gang-Gang:

> Believe in yourself and the strength of your convictions, and you will prevail.

> *What is your personal history? How does it affect your perceptions of events that happen today and your reactions to them?*

> *How does it affect your decisions?*

> *How does it affect your mindset?*

Stop here for a moment and write your Personal History in the form of an autobiography. Then examine it closely to determine how your personal history affects your mindset and your decision making style.

How did this happen?

What brought you to the decision to re-create yourself and change your life? At this point take a moment to look at the self-motivation that started you on this course or caused you to pick up this book.

I have been motivated to re-create myself many times. After I came to America I went right to work before achieving a college degree. This, despite the fact that my grandfather, Baba, had always maintained, "You need that piece of paper for credibility." But I did not have the money for tuition and there was no one available to provide guidance that I could finance my college degree with a school loan, or try to get a scholarship.

I continued to work at the types of jobs that did not require a college degree for some time. Since one of my dreams had been to be a model, I attended John Robert Powers' finishing school, and after graduation, I worked as a fashion model.

Another dream of mine was to be a Rock Star and so, I traveled the United States as a singer in a rock and roll band, recorded some music, and signed autographs, the works. In fact, I can still be heard as a vocalist on the better "oldies" radio stations.

I next worked as an executive assistant and then a systems analyst in the IBM midrange computer technology market and was successful at it. But soon enough, I learned that education was the ticket into the level of opportunity and compensation that I was struggling to attain.

By the time I decided to get a degree, I was a single parent with a small child and the only school I could afford was a local community college. I saved my money and each quarter took whatever classes I could within my field of study. I worked hard to excel in the adult academic setting and got an "A" in most of my classes. This wasn't easy since I worked all day and went to school at night, but I was motivated by a strong desire to succeed.

Eventually, I received my Associate of Applied Science in Computer Science degree. I was, of course, very proud of this achievement of another one of my dreams.

What it took

This achievement was not without some bumps in the road. While attending community college at night I worked for a large retail store chain as the Computer Operations Manager. This large, lucrative business emptied out a closet, installed a desk, and made it my office. Sometimes, my mean spirited colleagues called me "the girl in the closet," but I ignored them as I focused on learning my craft.

Once when it was time to leave for school at the end of the day, my manager told me "your education is not important" and insisted that I stay and work that night. Such statements did not deter me and I pressed on to completion of my college degree.

I established a deliberate plan for competency building and determined the best way for me to gain the desired skills, knowledge and experience to move into my new field. Then I used my new Associates degree to obtain a better position at a different company.

Wanting a better quality of life and a fulfilling career was why I decided to re-create myself at that time.

What was the impetus for your decision to recreate yourself?

How will you use what happened to you to make a change in your life?

Stop now for a few minutes and write down what event brought you to this crossroad and caused you to consider your self-creation or recreation.

Then follow up by evaluating the event, identifying your needs and wants, and measuring your progress towards creating and achieving new goals.

How do you recover?

Whatever the issue is that caused you to consider recreating yourself and your life, *now* is the time to decide how to recover.

After I received my AAS in Computer Science I still needed to rebuild my self-esteem from being "the girl in the closet." As I usually develop strong, mutually beneficial relationships in my personal and professional life, I checked my professional and social networks to determine what possibilities were available to me in my career.

I contacted a mentor and told him that I was prepared and ready to move from operations management to programming. As the Vice President of Information Technology who had always encouraged me to develop my skills in IT, and who already knew my work ethic and abilities, he offered me an entry-level position as a programmer. I would now move, it seemed, from being a manager, to starting over in a new whole new area.

This VP, Jim Kelly, was a godsend, and it was providence that he was in the market for a new programmer and the position was still open when I called. This situation provided me with the opportunity to change careers and hone my skills in a safe environment with someone who I already enjoyed a good relationship with.

With Jim's guidance and support I was able to recover from being "the girl in the closet" and develop a new career as a developer of software products.

What is the reality versus your perception of the situation?

Sometimes our perception of events is clouded by rationalizing the situation, while the reality is quite different from what is perceived, that which we're busily rationalizing.

I recall an occasion when I was a consultant in a global professional services firm and there was a colleague who communicated with me very erratically. Sometimes she would discuss personal issues with me and other times she would seem adversarial. I would work with her as best I could and thought we were making good progress toward a good level of communication. Then we were put on a project together where communication began to deteriorate rapidly.

One day during a meeting with another colleague, she began yelling and crying. I talked to her quietly and she only became more emotional, ran out of the room and slammed the door. Turning to the other manager in the room I wondered out loud what could be the problem. The manager replied, "Janet is really intimidated by you, didn't you know that?" I was stunned. I had no idea. While I was under the impression that she had personal problems, she was actually behaving that way because without my even realizing it, she found me intimidating.

So, determine what the reality is compared to your rationale or *perception* of the situation. You may be treating the wrong problem, or misreading the issue. Step back from the situation and evaluate it again, then check your premises to ensure the reality, and your perception of it, is based on fact.

What is your most pressing need as regards personal self-creation?

Are you concerned about your future marketability, your ability to get ahead in your career, or do you wish to position yourself for whole new options?

In other words, is your self-creation related to your career or to reaching self-actualization?

Your response to these questions will determine what your goals and plans should be.

If it is career related, do you wish to move into management and are not sure what the next steps should be? Or have you determined that you need more education to get to the next step.

Stay-at-home moms who are preparing to return to the job market for instance, undergo a process of self-creation to get back into the mindset required for working in corporate America. Typically they have been out of touch with the day-to-day requirements for their field, or advances in their area of focus have occurred.

Concentrate on the internal change first, because self-creation comes from the inside out. Be careful not to carve long-term plans in stone. Stay flexible and open to opportunities and possibilities.

It is better to concentrate on growth and keeping your options open, rather than locking into a hard and fast rule. This allows you to be open to the possibilities and event dynamics that may come your way. It also allows you to *recognize new opportunity* when it appears unexpectedly.

Keep your eyes on the target, stick to your guidelines, but stay flexible. Opportunities are often fleeting and require rapid decisions to take advantage of them.

Success is that place in the road where preparation and opportunity meet.

So keep your eyes and options open so that when opportunity comes, as it inevitably does, you will recognize it and seize it. If you hesitate, or are not flexible enough, it may take awhile before it comes around again.

Ask yourself: Why me? Why here? Why now? What lesson should I learn from this?

WHY ME? Look beyond the obvious.

There's a story about the two prisoners in one small cell with no light except what came through a tiny window three feet above eye level. Both prisoners spent a great deal of time looking at that window, of course.

One of them saw the bars—obvious, ugly, metallic reminders of reality. From day to day he grew increasingly discouraged, bitter, angry and hopeless.

By contrast, the other prisoner looked through the window to the stars and thought of the possibility of starting a new life in freedom.

The prisoners were looking at the same window, but one saw bars, while the other saw stars. And the difference in their *vision* made a huge difference in their lives.

Business leaders today are faced with a shortage of visionaries in the marketplace. "There are lots of 'nuts and bolts' people in business these days," they say, "people who will do exactly what they're told to do, exactly the way they are told to do it—no more, no less. There are plenty of robots, but precious few idea people. What we need is people with imagination, people who think overtime, who find ways to make improvements or increase efficiency."

Everything happens for a reason, the law of cause and effect. Sometimes we do not realize the reason immediately because it is not obvious. Perhaps it takes vision to recognize the answer to the question, Why Me?

Like the prisoner in the story you may think it is the worst thing that happened to you, when it is really the best thing that ever happened to you. You may see bars when you should see stars.

One of my mentors once told me, "Don't bring me problems, bring me solutions." Seeing stars instead of bars requires vision and helps you to find solutions.

Seeing Solutions instead of problems

Vision can be defined may ways. Let's discuss three.

Vision is the God given ability to see possible solutions to everyday problems of life.

Visionary people are solution oriented, not problem oriented. One way to do this is to *"Focus on Solutions."*

Reframing a Problem Often Leads To Its Solution

Reframing Example 1:

Have you ever noticed when driving under a bridge that there is information printed that tells truckers the acceptable height requirements for vehicles traveling under the bridge? An amusing story goes that one day a trucker, for reasons unknown, continued under a bridge that was lower than the load he was carrying.

The truck became lodged under the bridge halfway through and the driver found himself with the dilemma of how to get the truck unstuck. He called the office to notify them of what had happened, and soon several people were working on the problem.

The bridge where the truck had become stuck was right outside of a health facility where mentally ill people were housed and one of them had witnessed the incident. The patient watched through the bars in the fence for some time as several people discussed the situation and considered various options.

After awhile the patient said "I can help you solve the problem. I know how to get the truck out from under the bridge without further damage."

Everyone stopped what they were doing and all eyes fixed on the man behind the fence. "Oh yeah, how would you go about it?" asked the trucker.

"Let the air out of all of the tires," the patient replied, "Then the truck will be low enough to drive through, once the other side, you can re-inflate the tires and be on your way."

Everyone looked at each other, then set about the task of letting the air out of each tire. It worked!

"Wow! How did you think of that," they said to the patient.

"I'm crazy, not stupid" the patient replied.

Moral: The patient behind the fence was able to reframe the problem and thus saw a simple solution to what appeared to be a complex problem.

Reframing Example 2:

Many years ago, an architectural firm built a new and unique skyscraper. It was magnificent! This was one of the most innovative buildings that had ever been built. People were excited about the new materials and exciting architectural ideas that this new building offered.

There was only one problem. After the building was completed, the builders realized that they had neglected to install the elevator and now they had a major problem.

A janitor who was assigned to the clean up crew watched fascinated with curiosity as the architects pored over blueprints and held meetings and discussions regarding how to solve this problem.

Quietly the janitor said, "May I make a suggestion?"

All eyes turned on the janitor as the skeptical architects wondered how a janitor who knew nothing about blueprints or how to build skyscrapers could possibly have the solution to a problem that they, the experts, had been mulling over for days.

"What do you suggest?" the lead architect asked.

"Put the elevator on the outside of the building," replied the janitor.

"What a great idea!" they exclaimed.

The architects designed and built a beautiful glass enclosed elevator on the outside of the building and thus the first outside elevator was built.

Being encumbered by their concept of where elevators belonged in a building, the architects looked at where it should be instead of the possibilities of where it could be.

During your journey of self-creation, remember to *look at where you could be*, instead of *where you should be*.

Vision is not only for problem solving, of course. A second definition of vision is: **Vision is the ability to see beneath the surface.**

Visionaries know that it pays to look beyond the obvious to understand what makes things tick. Imagine everything that goes on in the ocean, every day. The surface can look very calm, but often just beneath the surface, there's an entire world of activity there.

Visionaries have an important mission to accomplish in their lives and the lives of others—looking past the obvious into the shadows, trying to draw out the greatness and the possibilities that exist in something or someone.

Vision offers you the ability to catch a glimpse of the possibilities for your life, as you open up to the abundance of the universe and practice visualization.

A critical component of self-creation is to be able to envision yourself as the person you wish to become. The subconscious mind does not have the ability to decipher what is real and what we are creating or visualizing for ourselves.

Therefore, one way to use the subconscious is *to act as if* you are already the person you wish to become. Then fix the picture of your new self in your mind and "*act as if*" you already *are* that person.

The subconscious mind will carry out its belief that you *are* that new person and people will begin to respond to you as if you already are that new you. Then one day you will realize that you have truly become that person you aspired to be and self-creation is complete.

Why Here? Why now?

I firmly believe that things happen when you are ready for them to happen. Don't get me wrong, now. I know that sometimes you think that you are not ready, or that this is not the right time. It is this feeling that triggers the questions, "why here, why now?

Be still, be very still and listen for the answer. It will come. One way to coax out the answer is to go through "self discovery."

Self-discovery

Self-discovery is the process of obtaining knowledge about one's self, such as motivations, history, or preferences that lead to the development of greater self-awareness.

I became increasingly frustrated at not being able to express what I wanted to convey in letters that I wrote, especially those to Mr. Elijah Muhammad. In the street, I had been the most articulate hustler out there—I had commanded attention when I said something. But now, trying to write simple English, I not only wasn't articulate, I wasn't even functional.

How would I sound writing in slang, the way I would *say* it, something such as "Look daddy, let me pull your cost about a cat, Elijah Muhammad—."

Many who today hear me somewhere in person, or on television, or those who read something I've said, will think I went to school far beyond the eighth grade. This impression is due entirely to my prison studies.

It had begun in the Charlestown Prison, when Bimbi first made me feel envy for his stock of knowledge. Bimbi had always taken charge of any conversation he was in, and I had tried to emulate him. But every book I picked up had few sentences which didn't contain anywhere from one to nearly all of the words that might as well have been in Chinese. Well I just skipped those words, of course. I really ended up with little idea of what the book said. So I had come to the Norfolk Prison Colony still going through only book-reading motions. Pretty soon, I would have quit even these motions, unless I had received the motivation that I did.

I saw that the best thing I could do was get hold of a dictionary—to study, to learn some words. I was lucky enough to reason also that I should try to improve my penmanship. It's sad. I couldn't even write in a straight line. It was both ideas together that moved me to request a dictionary along with some tablets and pencils from the Norfolk Prison Colony School.

I spent two days just riffling through the dictionary's pages. I'd never realized so many words existed! I didn't know *which* words I needed to learn. Finally, just to start some kind of action, I began copying.

In my slow, painstaking, ragged handwriting, I copied into my tablet everything printed on the first page, down to the punctuation marks.

I believe it took me a day. Then, aloud, I read back, to myself, everything I'd written on the tablet. Over and over, aloud, myself, I read my own handwriting.

I woke up the next morning, thinking about those words— immensely proud to realize that not only had I written so much at one time, but I'd written words whose meanings I didn't remember what many of these words meant. I reviewed the words whose meanings I didn't remember. Funny thing, from the dictionary first page right now, that "aardvark" springs to mind. The dictionary had a picture of it, a long-tailed, long eared, burrowing African mammal, which lives off termites caught by sticking out its tongue as an anteater does for ants.

I was so fascinated that I went on—I copied the dictionary's next page. And the same experience came when I studied that. With each succeeding page, I also learned of people and places and events from history. Actually the dictionary is like a miniature encyclopedia. Finally the dictionary's A section had filled a whole tablet—and I went into the B's. That was the way I started copying what eventually became the entire dictionary. It went a lot faster after so much practice helped to pick up handwriting speed. Between what I wrote in my tablet, and writing letters, during the rest of my time in prison, I would guess I wrote a million words.

I suppose that it was inevitable that as my word-base broadened, I could for the first time pick up a book and read and now begin to understand what the book was saying. Anyone who has read a great deal can imagine the new world that opened. Let me tell you something: from then until I left that prison, in every moment I had, if I was not reading in the library, I was reading on my bunk. You couldn't have gotten me out of books with a wedge. Between Mr. Muhammad's teachings, my correspondence, my visitors—usually Ella and Reginald—and my reading of books, months passed without my even thinking of being imprisoned. In fact, *up to then I had never been so truly free in all my life.* [emphasis added].

The Norfolk Prison Colony's library was in the school building. Instructors who came from such places as Harvard and Boston universities taught a variety of classes there. The weekly debates between inmate teams were also held in the school building. You would be astonished to know how worked up convict debaters and audiences would get over subjects like "Should Babies Be Fed Milk?"

Available on the prison library's shelves were books on just about every general subject. Much of the big private collection that Parkhurst had willed to the prison was still in crates and boxes in the back of the library—thousands of old books. Some of them looked ancient: covers faded, old-time parchment-looking binding. Parkhurst, I've mentioned, seemed to have been principally interested in history and religion. He had the money and the special interest to have a lot of books that you wouldn't have in general circulation. Any college library would have been lucky to get that collection.

As you can imagine, especially in a prison where there was heavy emphasis on rehabilitation, an inmate was smiled upon if he demonstrated an unusually intense interest in books. There was a sizeable number of well-read inmates, especially had popular debaters. Some were said by many to be practically walking encyclopedias. They were almost celebrities. No university would ask any student to devour literatures as I did when this new world opened to me, of being able to read and *understand*.

I read more in my room than in the library itself. An inmate who was known to read a lot could check out more than the permitted maximum number of books. I preferred reading in the total isolation of my own room.

When I had progressed to really serious reading, every night at about ten p.m., I would be outraged with the "lights out." It always seemed to catch me in the middle of something engrossing.

Fortunately, right outside my door was a corridor light that cast a glow into my room. The glow was enough to read by, once my eyes adjusted to it. So when "lights out" came, I would sit on the floor where I could continue reading in that glow.

At one-hour intervals the night guard paced past every room. Each time I heard footsteps approaching, I jumped into bed and feigned sleep. And as soon as the guard passed, I got right back onto the floor area of the light-glow, where I would read for another fifty-eight minutes—until the guard approached again. That went on until three or four in the morning. Three or fours hours of sleep a night was enough for me. Often in the years in the streets I had slept less than that."[1]

With self-awareness, initiative, and discovery of the possibilities that you can create for yourself, comes the freedom to reach and truly achieve self-actualization.

Identify your accomplishments:

It is crucial to your success at self-creation that you identify your strengths and accomplishments to date in order to:

- Build self-confidence (a key component to success)
- Build self-esteem
- Celebrate your ability to take charge of your life
- Realize that you are truly in control of who you are and your ability to become the new you

---

[1] Malcolm X with Alex Haley, *The autobiography of Malcolm X*

- Find a position with the best fit (if seeking a career option)
- Communicate effectively (at work or church or social events)
- Build bridges to the next level

An accomplishment is an activity which gives you pleasure, fulfillment and a feeling of success and achievement. It can be large or small in scope, happen frequently, or be something you have only done once, and be work related or personal. Accomplishments should reflect you at your best, sometimes by overcoming difficulties, and believing in yourself and your ideas. They are tangible proof that you possess a significant level of proficiency or expertise in a skill.

Now, looking over all that you have done in your life, select at least four to six accomplishments and describe them in detail. Use the accomplishment list below to describe them.

In your description of the event, try to elaborate on:

- What you did
- Where it happened
- When it occurred
- Why you did it
- How you did it
- What were the results
- How you felt when you achieved or accomplished it

After describing each achievement, analyze it. List the skills that enabled you to accomplish each task. Identify the skill sets used (i.e. those skills and personal characteristics that keep getting used again and again in accomplishment after accomplishment).

Your significant past experiences can be used to help you identify traits and skills that contribute to your success. It is these patterns that are helpful in choosing a future career, a life change, or career option.

The value gained from this exercise is to remind you not only of your accomplishments, but to rekindle the excited, even euphoric feeling of success that you experienced.

When writing these successes down, take note of how you feel during the process. Remember that feeling and do something physical while remembering the feeling of success.

The next time that you find yourself feeling like you cannot do something, or you are not a success in life, recall the memory of this success to help you through and as supportive evidence that you have already been successful.

Before you can unlock the future, you must first find the keys to your past.

Accomplishment List

Accomplishment: # _____

Situation/Problem:

_____
_____
_____
_____
_____

Action Taken:

_____
_____
_____
_____
_____

Results:

_____
_____
_____
_____
_____

Skills Used:

_____   _____   _____
_____   _____   _____

Use this Worksheet to identify your accomplishments to date.
Make as many copies of the sheet as necessary to chronicle them all. You
may find you have accomplished much more than you realize.

Chapter Two

Principle Two

Realize that this is not a crisis—It's the beginning of a great adventure

We cannot tell what may happen to us in the strange medley of life. But we can decide what happens in us, how we take it, what we do with it—and that is what really counts in the end.
Joseph Fort Newton

Chapter Two

We cannot tell what may happen to us in the strange medley of life. But we can decide what happens in us, how we take it, what we do with it—and that is what really counts in the end.

Joseph Fort Newton

Realize that this is not a crisis—It's the beginning of a great adventure

Personal Mastery—It's going to be a thrill ride

Many people say that personal mastery is the learning system that they are most drawn to because they want to reach their potential. Mastery involves not only producing results but to "master" the principles underlying the way the results are produced. This is because in mastering themselves there is a sense of joyousness that comes from the ability and willingness to understand and work with the forces around them.

Personal mastery involves learning to create and keep not just a personal vision, but a clear picture of your current reality. By doing this, you generate a force within yourself that is called "creative tension." Since tension by nature seeks resolution, and the most natural resolution for this tension is to move closer to what you want, it is as though in so doing, you set up two poles, one of your vision and one of your reality.

If you are convinced that your vision and the result are important, you will see clearly that you must change your life in order to attain your vision. That in order to attain your vision, you must commit yourself to the results while still maintaining a sense of deliberate patience with yourself and the world around you.

Some people think, "I will never be able to accomplish my vision, because of the way I was raised. I know I will never get or have what I want." Or they may say, "I will only be able to force myself towards my vision if things get bad enough." Or even, "I will have to push ahead through sheer willpower against all the obstacles thrown at me." These are all fears that are manifested by "emotional tension" operating on basic beliefs that you are unworthy or powerless to achieve your deepest aspirations. To cope with this tension accept that it exists and try to see it more clearly. Recognize that this is just emotional tension and it is a natural part of your reality.

To achieve personal mastery on the road to self-creation, do not lower your personal vision, even if it seems as if the vision is impossible. The content of the personal vision is not important in and of itself. You see, it is not what the vision *is* but what the vision *does* that is important. Stories abound of people who achieve extraordinary results with extraordinary visions and the results are different from their original intent.

Personal mastery will enable you to embrace seeing the world as it is, even when it makes you feel uncomfortable. Looking closely and honestly at your current reality is one of the most difficult tasks on the road to self-creation. The effort in "facing reality" teaches you to choose what you want, and the choosing is a very courageous act, because it means picking the results and actions that you will fashion into your personal destiny. Practicing self-creation is like holding a conversation with yourself. One inner voice dreams of what you wish to become for the future while another casts an often baleful eye on the world around you. A third voice, often deeper down inside, will say, "I have chosen what I want and accepted that I will create it." When Jeff Bezos envisioned an online bookstore where people would come to find all of their favorite books, it might have seemed far-fetched. But today, Amazon.com leads the way in online bookstores and this new business model.

It is important to hear all of these voices and understand their facets clearly, knowing that the power that propels you towards your vision emerges from the relationship between all of your inner voices.

So Tell Me—What do you really want?

Now you must define your personal vision, what you want to create for yourself and the world around you. Since a personal vision and self-creation requires commitment, and because it profoundly affects and influences your decisions going forward, it should not be taken lightly. You will need to do self-examination at a level that you may have never done before. If you stick to it and follow through, however, you will see how powerful that answer to the question, "but what do you really want", can be.

Key One: Create a result

Start in a reflective frame of mind and recall an image of something memorable to you. It could be anything or anytime you felt something special was happening to you. Then imagine a result in your life that you deeply desire. For example, it may be getting an advanced degree, or owning a home in a neighborhood where you most want to live, or having the relationship that you most desire, or losing weight, or even writing a book.

Do not focus on whether your vision is possible or not. Instead, imagine yourself accepting into your life, the full manifestation of the result.

Describe in writing or by drawing a picture the experience you have just imagined, using the past tense, as if it has already happened.

What does it look like?

_____

_____

_____

_____

What does it feel like?

_____

_____

_____

How would you describe it to someone else?

_____

_____

_____

_____

Key Two: Reflect on the vision you just articulated

Pause for a moment and consider what you answered to the question "what does it look like?" Is your vision close to what you really wanted to create for yourself? If not, there may be many reasons why it manifested the way it did.

For example: *It doesn't matter what I want*—Some people assume that what they want is not important. Do not belittle yourself. If you have doubts, then imagine what you would want if you actually did deserve it.

Last year at a conference I met a woman who set aside her dreams for decades because she thought that everyone else in the family had to come first.

She focused on taking the kids to their games and pretty much became their private taxi service. She put her husband first and used that to set aside her own dreams as she said yes to anyone who ever asked her a favor. It was as if she did not have the ability to say no to anyone but herself. Soon she found that she was always very tired and realized that she never had any time for herself.

We had a chance encounter as we entered a workshop together and during our conversation she made a statement that so intrigued me, I had to have her share it with you. Here's what she told me in an interview:

> I decided 5 years ago to live for myself instead of living for others. What I mean by that is, I defined myself by how others perceived me and what they thought I ought to be doing. And I worked hard to meet that criteria or that image of those things that people wanted me to do. And I didn't stop to think about what it is that I want.
>
> It started when I had my children and all the things that occur when you are a mom and what a mom is supposed to be. That meant even making career decisions relative to the kind of flexibility that I thought that I needed in order to do a number of things so that I could stay with myself because I thought it was important.
>
> Now I understand what I had actually done, because it happens quite frequently and I think we've all done that at some point or to some extent regardless of who we are.

I said, "What I'm really interested in is this. What have you found since you started this new way of living?"

> A couple of things. One is, my relationship with my family has improved. This happened because my own self-esteem has risen considerably since I made this decision. Now when I am asked something I consider it against all the other things that I may or may not have wanted to do. Whereas in the past, I would have immediately set aside what I had planned to do or what I'm thinking through and immediately go towards what they wanted to do.
>
> My family and I also have better conversations because they realize that its important that they understand my viewpoint and the way I do things, and it's not always the way they look at something or their viewpoint on the topic. I speak up more about what I want, whereas in the past I thought that meant being aggressive and now I understand it means being heard. It means being assertive and there's a difference. So that is when I started my own company.

I asked her, "And so, what do you think about being a business owner? How's it going?"

> It's going very well, and it's going very well because I defined my criteria for success. When I started I embraced a lot of the information that's available about what success means and how you define success. And this is what you should have to live a good life, etc., etc. Then I finally realized that I define my good life, and what's good for me, and what it is that I want to accomplish. So what if someone wants to talk to me about gross revenues. I ask them why do they need that because that has absolutely nothing to do with the goals for my business and the vision I want for my business.
>
> What I want for my business, what I use as my measurement of success is how I relate more to people. I ask them "what kind of things are you doing now?" You know, "what kind of interesting things are you doing in your business?"
>
> I'm more interested in having conversations around . . . well just let me say that now most of my colleagues are people that I call and hear conversations around what they are doing now. Or, you've got to hear what I'm doing now because this is really interesting and I know you and I talked about this months ago, so let me tell you how it turned out.

I asked her if she would you be willing to write an article once in awhile for my website from that perspective and she responded that she had never been asked to write an article before. So this was an opportunity for her to grow.

Kay's idea of success is based on her own measurement criteria, which is constantly growing, "because I'm always seeking, I'm always looking and I like sharing. So my success is when a client understands something new for himself or herself, and then they turn around and can share something with me. That is my success. My success is not doing $50 to $100 thousand with the client. My success is different. So that's why what I do continually grows; it's not static. In fact it helps me define what I do because you'll meet me six months later and I'm not necessarily doing that particular thing."

I asked if she would you describe her method as "to just open yourself up to the universe and what it feels like bringing to you."

Kay responded, "Absolutely. There are two definitions from Nike that says no fear. I'm sure for them it's defined from the athletic perspective, but I took it from the spiritual level: in terms of the universe is open for us all and it's up to us to literally pick and choose where we want to go, what we want to do with it, how we want to embrace it. And you know, consequences are sometimes handcuffs for people. Because they dwell way too much on the consequences to open themselves up to the endless possibilities."

That perspective is exactly why I asked her for this interview, because she's got one of the secrets of success.

You must define what success means to you in order to apply the right criteria when determining if you are a success or not. Only you have the secret that has you getting up every day and saying, "Yes, it's going to be a good day."

My reply to Kay was just this: "The very words you have said to me embody the secret. 'I decided to be true to myself and live my life on my own terms and I measure my success not from any other perspective than my own definition, and here's what it is.' That's exactly what's in my new book "Self Creation: 10 Powerful Principles for Changing Your Life", and you said those words to me in passing and I knew I had to interview you. I believe that there are no coincidences. You see, I had left the building, and I turned around and came all the way back, thinking that I was going to enter one of the seminars and instead I ran into you and started talking with you. Then when you said those words to me I realized that's what I really came back for. I came back to meet you, I didn't know it, but that's why I really came back."

"You know, it was as if there was some divine intervention. The words that embody what the book is about and to have you talk about the possibilities, coming from you when I just met you, it's kismet, or destiny or something like that. It's Syncropurpose, as Robert Pino who wrote the book "Absolute Victory", would call it."

This book came to me in my car. The whole book came to me then. Every single chapter, and indeed, all I've been doing is plugging in the chapters behind the outline that I conceived in the car that day. And that is when I started carrying a tape recorder with me. Because I was going, "Oh my God, I don't have a pen, I don't want to lose this idea." Ideas are so fragile and fleeting so I didn't want to lose this one. When I got home, I showed my family what I had scribbled in the car and my son said "that sounds like a really good idea."

I explained all this to Kay, who added that, "I admire people who can write."

"Well you can too," I quipped, "and I'm going to hold you to your word that you will write an article for the newsletter." We closed the interview on that note, but I'll just say that everyone should look for writings and articles from Kay Herring of Goodwin Grier Consulting on my site in the future.

You see, it does matter what you want, and Kay Herring is living proof that if you follow what you want, the universe will work in your favor to help you to attain it.

I want what someone else wants—Some people base their vision on what they think other people, such as a parent, spouse or their children, want for them.

The great Brian Tracy says "Refuse to make excuses. The opposite of accepting responsibility is making excuses, blaming others and becoming upset, angry and resentful toward people for what they have done to you or not done for you."

Any one of these three behaviors can trip you up and be enough to cost you the game:

If you run into an obstacle or setback and you make excuses rather than accept responsibility, it's a five-yard penalty. It can cost you a first down. It can cost you a touchdown. It can make the difference between success and failure.

If, when you face a problem or setback, and you both make excuses and blame someone else, you get a 10-yard penalty. In a tightly contested game, where the teams are just about even, a 10-yard penalty can cost you the game.

If, instead of accepting responsibility when things go wrong, you make excuses, blame someone else and simultaneously become angry and resentful and blow up, you get a 15-yard penalty. This may cost you the championship and your career as well if it continues.

Remember, when you envision the result you should include it only *if that is what you want for yourself.*

I can't have what I want—Some people find that imagining a vision contradicts thoughts and feelings held since childhood. Or they may feel that they have to trade off against something else such as, either a successful career or a satisfying family life.

There are two things you can do immediately to change your thinking and put your ideas into action.

First, be completely honest and realistic with yourself and every difficult situation that enters your life. Resolve to face the truth, no matter what it is. Don't just wish, hope, pray, ignore or play games with yourself.

Second, accept complete responsibility for your life, especially when things go wrong. Refuse to blame others or make excuses. Your strength of character shows when you are under pressure. So be calm, controlled and constructive at all times and allow yourself to think it through. Be open so that you are able to recognize not only what you want, but that you *can* have what you want.

I really don't know what I want—In that case, suppose you had a vision of greatness. What would that be? A vision exists within everyone even if we are unable to articulate it. A reluctance to articulate vision is a measure of your despair and suggests a reluctance to take responsibility for your own life.

A vision statement is an expression of hope, and without hope it is difficult to create a vision.

When President Kennedy announced his vision to "put a man on the moon . . . within the next ten years," it not only sounded exceedingly challenging, but seemed like an impossible dream. In those days people would look up in the sky and say it was impossible.

Undeterred by naysayers, John F. Kennedy not only articulated his vision statement, but also gave the team a timeline in which to accomplish this feat. On schedule, a man did walk on the moon and the whole world watched as our world of possibilities was changed forever. The event was such an unreal one that people all over the world stopped what they were doing, and became glued to their television as they watched and waited breathlessly for the astronauts to not only land on the moon, but to return to Earth safely.

Today, what seemed impossible when John F. Kennedy expressed his vision statement barely gets a yawn, as manned space stations are not merely a normal occurrence, but sometimes the passenger is not even an astronaut.

I am afraid of what I want—Some people fear letting themselves want anything because they think it may get out of control and they will be forced to change their lives. Remember, this is *your* vision, you control it, and it can only increase your self-awareness.

Don't be afraid to step out of your comfort zone and achieve your wildest dreams. You will find that it makes you free as you realize that not only are you able to achieve it, but it brings you a strong feeling of accomplishment and enhances your self esteem.

I already know what I want—You may create anything you wish, but remember that a personal vision is not a done deal already existing and waiting for you to find it. *This is something you create and continue to recreate your whole life—a process rather than an event.*

When I first arrived in the United States from Jamaica, all I wanted was to achieve the American Dream. At the time this meant a good job, a plot of land with a home to call my own and other outward trappings of success that I had hungered for while growing up on the island.

After I had achieved what, while still in Jamaica I would have considered "a good job", I found that my personal vision changed and I wanted to achieve a college education.

After I had an Associate of Applied Science degree, I was bitten by the educational bug and liked what had become of me as I became a transformational learner. Naturally, I now needed a Bachelor of Arts degree, and so I had already set my sights on my next achievement. Though this next goal was not accomplished until after my 50th birthday, I refused to use age as an excuse on the way to its achievement.

Soon I dreamed of having my own company and found myself focused on all that that dream entailed!

None of it is easy, by no means, but the point is that you will continually evolve beyond each achievement and as each of your dreams are realized.

I know what I want, but I can't have it at work—Some people think that even by thinking about it and bringing those thoughts to the surface, they may jeopardize their current jobs. This stops them from articulating their vision.

This question of the current reality is worth testing. If this is true, then your self-creation may involve finding a different place to work, which supports your vision to flourish and grow.

Key Three: Describe your personal vision

Answer the following questions. If these categories do not fit you and your needs, adjust them accordingly. Work through all of them until you can see a complete picture of what you want.

Visualization helps you to achieve the life that you truly, deeply desire. As you visualize, ask yourself what your personal vision looks like. What does it feel like? What words would you use to describe it?

What is your self-image: If you could be exactly the kind of person you always wanted to be what qualities would you have?

_____

_____

_____

_____

Identify the tangibles—What material things would like to own?

_____

_____

_____

_____

Visualize your home—What is your ideal living environment like?

_____

_____

_____

_____

Health and well-being—What do you desire for your health, fitness and anything to do with your body?

_____

_____

_____

_____

Personal relationships—What types of relationship would you like to have with friends, family and others?

_____

_____

_____

_____

Work life—Describe your ideal professional or vocational environment. How would you like to impact your company and those around you?

_____
_____
_____
_____

Identify Personal Pursuits—Describe what you want to create in the area of personal and individual learning, domestic and global travel, reading and other activities.

_____
_____
_____
_____

Community—Describe your vision for the community you live in or for society as a whole.

_____
_____
_____
_____

Is there anything else or any other area of your life that you would like to create or change? If so write it down here.

_____
_____
_____
_____

Your Life Purpose—Visualize that your life has a unique purpose that is fulfilled by what you do, your inter-relationships and the way you choose to live it. Describe your unique purpose as another part of your vision and aspiration.

_____
_____
_____
_____

Key 4—Expand on and Clarify the Vision

Most people begin this exercise with a mixture of selfless and self-centered components. Then they begin to wonder, "Is it alright to want fine cars, diamonds and a luxury mansion?" Remember, this exercise enables you to suspend your judgment about what is 'worthy' of being your vision so that you can ask yourself *"which aspect of this vision is closest to my deepest desires?"* This allows you to expand or clarify the dimensions of your vision.

At this point you can now review the components of your vision from self-image, home, health, relationships, work, personal desires, community, life purpose or anything else you feel is important. Take each component individually and answer each question before moving on to the next one:

If I could have it now, would I take it?

Assuming I have it now, what has it brought me?

These two questions move your vision into a richer focus allowing you to see its underlying implications more clearly. Suppose you visualized a sports car in front of your new mansion. Why do you want them? What does it allow you to do? "Well," you may reply, "to experience freedom and security." But why do you want freedom and security?

The point of asking these follow up questions is to discover what your true desires are and what the motivation is that shaped and created this as your vision. You may discover that your stress filled job invokes feelings of being trapped and you really want to have more freedom to enjoy other aspects of life.

Figuring out all aspects of your vision takes time. Think of it like peeling back the layers of an onion where each removed layer reveals more value as you gain a clearer understanding of what you really want from life. As you remove each layer, ask yourself: "If I could have it now, would I take it? If I had it now, what would it bring me?"

You may find that each component of your personal vision leads you to the same place. Each of us has our own set of goals, but sometimes they are buried so deep that when we examine them through this exercise, we may be brought to tears by the awareness of what has driven us in life. Keep asking the question, "What would it bring to me?" and immerse yourself in this insistent structure that forces you to take the time to see what you clearly and deeply desire. You may discover that it is good to finally have a clear personal vision and all you have to do is execute the necessary steps to implement it.

Be prepared. Prepare yourself for change and its effects on your perception of who you are and what you have to offer.

Be careful not to convince yourself that everything is totally under your control and will not change. Quite the contrary, be prepared for lots of change. A butterfly goes through a metamorphosis that may look slow and dreary, but in the end it emerges as one of the most beautiful creatures of nature.

Mark's Story

As anyone who has been a project manager can tell you, regardless of how well organized you and your team may be or how much planning you do, change is the only thing you can be sure of. Sometimes you can follow all the rules and methodology, have all of your ducks lined up in a row, and still be blindsided by unexpected surprises.

One particular project comes to mind where a new project manager was brought in to execute a project recovery. He knew the methodology, had great communications skills and loved working with people. The team worked hard and soon reached a synergy that brought great pride to the champions, ambassadors, and executive sponsors who were involved with the project. This high performance team was humming along when they reached a point in the project where they needed to raise awareness in the field about next steps, and how each corporate location would benefit from the new system.

All was well until a key player on the team decided to focus on development of the product demo for the outlying locations, instead of focusing on the work at hand. Soon the project began to slip. When the project manager communicated this to his client counterpart, the response was, "Our organizational culture is such that we prefer not to rock the boat as regards employees. The project is going well, the team has jelled and is performing well, and I am satisfied that we will make our deadline."

Two weeks later, the project sponsor brought in a third party to audit the project. It was noted that the project was falling behind schedule and that the team seemed to have veered off into focusing on delivering demonstrations to the outlying locations at the expense of planned tasks.

The team had no responsibility for the project slip, since it is the project manager's responsibility, and the client project manager was reluctant to admit that he had made the decision to not "rock the boat." The project manager was found liable for not escalating the issue of slippage to the executive sponsor and he was promptly removed from the project and a project administrator hired to replace him.

Completely blindsided, he never saw it coming. He wondered how this could have happened when he had done such a great job and cared so much for his team and his client's well being. He soon found out that there was a reason why the illusion had ended.

Mark thought he wanted to be a project manager, but what he found out was that his talents lay elsewhere. As new opportunities came his way, he found himself moving into a whole new career. He began teaching MBA students about what it was like to be a consultant. He reveled in it and spared them no effort. He taught them the joys and the horrors of being a consultant.

"As a consultant," he told them, "you are sent anywhere in the country or in some instances anywhere in the world they wish to send you, and into all types of corporations. Each corporation has a different organizational culture and you have to adapt quickly if you are to succeed."

"You must identify the champion of your project, manage expectations and get work done through people who do not report to you. You must stay out of the politics of the organization while being cognizant of who the players are and where potential landmines are buried."

"You have to be aware of different communication styles and develop the ability to hear the unspoken, and to correctly translate the spoken. All this without becoming a casualty of the environment, while being the champion of your corporate sponsor and your consulting firm."

His students, who were from all over the world, listened earnestly and some decided then and there *not* to become consultants since, in their estimation, it was too difficult to control. The idea of so much travel away from their families was too demanding for some, and they thanked him for being so honest about the profession. A few, though, found Marks description to be fascinating and looked forward with anticipation to joining the ranks of the consultants in that exciting field.

As this, the third career for Mark materialized, he found himself getting opportunities to be a professional speaker. He was even interviewed on television as an expert in the area of career change. Before long, he was hosting his own television show to help the disadvantaged achieve their career dreams.

More recently, Mark began getting offers for speaking engagements for Internet topics and he's once again in the limelight as an expert in his field.

All of these achievements came to him *after* he was removed from the project. You see, sometimes what seems like a crisis is really the opportunity of a lifetime. Perhaps unexpected things happen because it is an inevitable part of the transition from one career to another or from one life event to another. Keep that in mind as you prepare for and experience your self-creation, for its positive effects may be around a corner.

Cheryl's Story

Cheryl was a singer in a rock and roll band. She loved it! She was living a dream come true.

Cheryl started singing when she was only 3 years old. She always loved to sing, and one day at Sunday school her grandmother put her up on the stage to say a little poem:

> *"Flowers on my shoulders,*
> *Slippers on my feet,*
> *I am mommies darling,*
> *Don't you think I'm sweet?"*

The crowd broke into applause, as she beamed with joy and a twinkle in her eyes. Right then and there the audience knew, as did she, that she had found something she loved.

Soon Cheryl was singing at birthday parties and gained a small reputation as a good little singer.

She filed it all away in the back of her mind and promised herself that one day she would be a singer and people would pay to see her perform on stage.

With hard work and persistence, Cheryl eventually achieved her dream. Anyone can, provided they have faith in themselves, the courage to write down and pursue their dream, and the wisdom and strength to press on, regardless of their inner fears.

So expanding on and clarifying the vision is an important component of success. Cheryl knew she wanted to be a singer, but it was only through self-reflection that she realized that it all came from that one moment in Sunday school so many years ago.

Mark thought he wanted to be a project manager, but learned that he was much better as a trainer and actually liked teaching more than managing projects.

Like the butterfly who must go through a painful transformation in the cocoon before reaching the height of its beauty, so you too must decide to do whatever it takes in order to achieve your vision.

The key is to never give up and focus on the possibilities and on your dreams, because when they come true, as they inevitably will, it will be one of the great moments of your life.

Chapter 3

Principle Three

Evaluate Yourself and Vision— Do a Gap Analysis

Mark Twain may have put it best when he said, "Inherently, each one of us has the substance within to achieve whatever our goals and dreams define. What is missing from each of us is the training, education, knowledge and insight to utilize what we already have."

Chapter 3

Mark Twain may have put it best when he said, "Inherently, each one of us has the substance within to achieve whatever our goals and dreams define. What is missing from each of us is the training, education, knowledge and insight to utilize what we already have."

Evaluate Yourself and Vision—Do a Gap Analysis

Gap analysis examines the difference between the current state and the desired state and helps to "bridge the gap" to achieving the new one.

Try on the new you or the new career before you make the change.

Evaluate whether you need more specialized skills or certification in a new skill to succeed in your new career or to achieve your vision.

Quite often when thinking of a career or life change the responsibilities of the new position are unknown. There are several methods currently used by corporations that enable employees to "try on" a position before making the career change. For example, you can "shadow" someone who works in the field you wish to move to thus enabling you to see what a typical day or week is like in that job.

Indeed, this style of checking out a career first is a good idea if you are not quite sure which position is right for you. Sometimes by doing this you find at closer inspection that the job is nothing like you thought it was, or that the requirements are such that further education or longer work hours are required. This "shadowing" method allows you to see in advance what the job is really like without having to give up your current position.

Sometimes additional training or certification is required for a successful career move and it behooves the person making the career change to do a thorough investigation prior to executing this strategy and making the investment of time and money.

Your company may be prepared to pay for your training since your improved skills will benefit both you and the company. In order for companies to remain competitive in the marketplace they also need a workforce with up-to-date skills. Similarly, benefits like additional training cuts down on attrition, which can be very costly to businesses.

Another alternative is to seek out a mentor who already works in the field of interest and spark a conversation to determine the subtle characteristics required for the position. For example, a developer who is considering moving to call center work may find that interaction with the public in a customer service role is not compatible with their personality. Whereas a continued role in the development area, moving to architect of a software module for instance, more naturally suits their personality and style of working.

Each individual must find their own motivation and determine whether the desire to change careers is based on sound reasoning.

Among other things, you need to verify whether you are in the wrong career or if the motivation to change careers is based solely on monetary compensation or because something is amiss in your personal interactions or personal life.

Prior to executing a career change I suggest that you put together a list of your career expectations.

Use the Career Expectations Worksheet at the end of this chapter to focus your expectations.

Create a list of things you really enjoy about your current career. If you have difficulty filling this list, it may indeed be time for a career change.

Put together a list of things you would like in your career where the needs are currently unmet in your current position.

Look around your present company to see what position could potentially provide you with more job satisfaction. Then go through the process again to see if the job is what you think it is.

The man who worked real hard but found himself unhappy

I am reminded of an attorney who worked hard to pass the bar exam, then worked even harder to make partner, only to find himself asking, "Is this all there is? Why am I not happy?"

Thousands of dollars later, he and his psychiatrist realized that he was an attorney because all the men in his family had been attorneys and that was what his family expected of him from the day he was born. What he really wanted to do, he realized, was work with children.

He made a drastic career change and found that he was much happier. While his income was not at the same level as before, he experienced a tremendous feeling of accomplishment. He had found his calling.

Career change can be a daunting and yet very rewarding process. Rewarding because you are challenged and excited about learning and using new skills and abilities. Daunting because you may have to begin at an entry-level position again and have to work your way back to your present level of expertise or compensation.

Sometimes it takes a step backwards in order to go forwards

I remember once when a new computer hardware system entered the marketplace and I wanted to get my hands on that system more that anything. I took a 25% cut in pay to get on the new system and learn it, but a year later, I had almost doubled my salary. Why? Because the skills required for the new system were scarce and the market was paying premium wages for those new skills. A more current example might be today's market for Web development or network technology skills.

One thing's for sure, if you want to change careers, you must make a plan and work through it. Like anything else, you will need to set your goals, do your research, create a plan and follow the steps to achievement of your goals.

You must:

➤ Plan your mission. What career do you wish to move to?

_____
_____
_____
_____

➤ Visualize and articulate your career goal.

_____
_____
_____
_____

➤ Plan the steps necessary to reach the certifications and skills required.

_____
_____
_____
_____

➢ Set personal deadlines for steps toward achievement of your new career goal.

_____

_____

_____

_____

➢ Benchmark your progress along the way. What is your benchmark plan?

_____

_____

_____

_____

➢ Remember that preparation always precedes success. Failure to plan is planning to fail. What is your plan?

_____

_____

_____

_____

According to Tom Peters, today's employee will go through at least 3 career changes in their lifetime. Perhaps now is the time for one of yours.

One avenue might be, when a new project is being launched that provides some of the new skills you need, make certain that you offer yourself to the project team. This is a particularly useful approach, incidentally, for those in the technology fields. In these new eCommerce/Internet times, everything changes so rapidly that in order for those in the field of technology to remain viable and employable, they must constantly upgrade their skills to stay abreast with the reality of new technology, inventions and of the new economy.

To benefit from a successful change, you have to:

1. Set goals
2. Measure your progress towards those goals
3. Make adjustments as necessary to achieve your goals
4. Work your plan, to achieve a smooth transition to your new career.

Next, Do a Gap Analysis

Gap Analysis (Delta analysis) is used when we want to change the way things are now to the way we want things to be. Delta (Δ) is the Greek symbol for change. To utilize this type of analysis we define the difference between the two states and identify the steps necessary to get from "the way things are" to "the way we want things to be."

To demonstrate this mode, see the Gap Analysis graphic below as an example of your current situation.

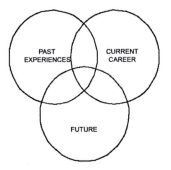

When we bring the circles together and allow them to partially overlap, we preserve some of the past and some of the present. This overlap helps us to preserve and reuse some of the present skills and knowledge in our expectations for the future.

Do the following to execute a Gap analysis regarding your current situation:

1. Evaluate your past experiences and identify the skills and talents that enabled you to achieve personal growth and that you currently use in your career.
2. Evaluate your current career and identify skills and knowledge that can be transferred from simple learning into transformative learning.

   o Simple learning is knowledge or skills only.

3. Determine how these talents, knowledge and skills can be transferred from simple learning into transformative learning.

   o Transformative learning is synonymous with growth and will be used to help convert your present credentials to the credentials required for the new career or your personal vision.

CAREER EXPECTATIONS WORKSHEET

Ask yourself these questions:

1. If I could have any job I want, what would it be?

_____
_____
_____
_____
_____
_____

2. What will it provide me with?

_____
_____
_____
_____
_____
_____

3. What kind of tasks would I perform?

_____
_____
_____
_____
_____
_____

4. What size organization do I want to work in?

_____
_____
_____
_____
_____
_____

6. Do I want to be a big fish in a little pond? Or a little fish in a big pond?

_____
_____
_____
_____
_____

6. What type of people do I enjoy working with?

_____
_____
_____
_____
_____
_____

7. How dynamic an environment would suit my taste?

_____
_____
_____
_____
_____
_____

8. Do I like to work on the bleeding edge or the leading edge of the field?

_____
_____
_____
_____
_____
_____

9. Do I prefer to interact with the functional groups, or work where I stay more technical?

_____
_____
_____
_____
_____
_____

10. Do I prefer working in global or local situations?

_____
_____
_____
_____
_____
_____
_____

11. Do I want to work cross culturally with other countries or only in the U.S.?

_____
_____
_____
_____
_____
_____

12. Do I have the diversity and cross-cultural skills required to work with other countries?

_____
_____
_____
_____
_____
_____

13. Do I want to travel? If so, how much travel?

_____
_____
_____
_____
_____

14. Am I willing to move to another state?

_____
_____
_____
_____
_____
_____

15. Am I willing to move to another country?

_____
_____
_____
_____
_____

If the answer to 15 is yes, continue with these questions . . .

16. What are my expectations for working in a foreign country?

_____

_____

_____

_____

_____

_____

17. Have I made a list of my goals? What are my long term and short-term goals?

_____

_____

_____

_____

_____

_____

18. What are my hidden (or unspoken) expectations?

_____

_____

_____

_____

_____

_____

19. What cultural experiences can I expect from working abroad?

_____

_____

_____

_____

_____

_____

20. How will this experience impact my objectives?

_____

_____

_____

_____

_____

_____

21. What will help me prepare and get the most out of my organizational experience abroad?

_____
_____
_____
_____
_____
_____

22. How familiar am I with my own cultural heritage?

_____
_____
_____
_____
_____

23. Write 5 goals and/or expectations for living and working in another culture or for your personal vision results.

_____
_____
_____
_____
_____
_____
_____
_____
_____
_____
_____
_____
_____
_____
_____

Now consider how you plan to achieve those 5 goals.

Will you need assistance? If so, identify who can assist you.

What is your plan to meet and work with those who can assist you in achieving these 5 goals?

_____
_____
_____
_____
_____
_____
_____
_____
_____
_____
_____
_____
_____
_____
_____
_____
_____

Chapter 4

Principle Four

Achievement of Your Dreams is Possible

Until one is committed, there is hesitancy, the chance to draw back, always ineffectiveness. Concerning all acts of initiative and creation, there is one elementary truth the ignorance of which kills countless ideas and splendid plans.

At the moment one definitely commits one's self then providence moves too, all sorts of things occur to help one that would never have occurred otherwise. A whole stream of events issues from the decision, raising in one's favor all manner of unforeseen incidents and meetings and material assistance which no man would have dreamed would have come his way. Whatever you can do, or dream you can, begin it. Boldness has Genius, Power and Magic in it. Begin it now.

Gerte

Chapter 4

Until one is committed, there is hesitancy, the chance to draw back, always ineffectiveness. Concerning all acts of initiative and creation, there is one elementary truth the ignorance of which kills countless ideas and splendid plans

At the moment one definitely commits one's self then providence moves too, all sorts of things occur to help one that would never have occurred otherwise. A whole stream of events issues from the decision, raising in one's favor all manner of unforeseen incidents and meetings and material assistance which no man would have dreamed would have come his way. Whatever you can do, or dream you can, begin it. Boldness has Genius, Power and Magic in it. Begin it now.

Gerte

Achievement of Your Dreams is Possible

When the moment arrives, you may have to learn to do new things.

I never needed to learn how to cook or be a housekeeper; I had always had a maid and a cook and I went to the best schools on the island. I always got what I wanted and life, for me, was more like easy street.

It sounds nice doesn't it? Well don't let the sound of it fool you. It is nice to have a cook and a maid, the only trouble is you grow up not knowing how to do these things yourself because someone else does them for you.

When my precious Gang-Gang went to America I learned how important it is to be able to do those tasks for myself. With no one caring for me, I was unable to cook for myself when the moment arrived, and I soon realized the importance of knowing how to do such things. Upon her return from America,

Gang-Gang set about the task of teaching me how to take care of myself and I discovered that I loved cooking.

At one point while still at Immaculate Conception High, I decided I wanted to be a nun. I was so sure that was what I wanted that I asked for permission to become one. You see, I was so young at the time that a guardian needed to sign for me. When I asked Gang-Gang to do this she told me, "Wait until you are old enough to sign for yourself, and if you still wish to become a nun, then you have my blessing."

When the time came and I was old enough to sign for myself, I said, "Become a nun, are you crazy? I want to date and have fun!" Gang-Gang was a wise woman indeed.

Immaculate Conception High

Going to a Catholic all girls high school has its benefits, but you learn little about interacting with boys and dating skills there. Couple that with a very protective environment at home and you have a young woman who does not interact well with peers of the opposite sex, lacking the opportunities to learn these particular social skills.

I muddled through my mistakes, but luckily had been raised with the ethics and values of Gang-Gang and Ba-Ba, which saved me from making unprincipled decisions or any truly serious errors of judgment.

America

The dream of going to America was seventeen years old when my visa finally came through. Filled with excitement I readied myself to reach the shores of the country where "the streets are paved with gold."

It was April when I arrived and still very cold at New York's LaGuardia Airport. Exiting the plane I was a seventeen year old dreamer in a big floppy hat, high-heeled pumps, and a pink sheath with sheer pink organza coat. I shivered in the cold wind and sought out the mother I could only recall having seen once in my life.

My mother had brought a lovely leopard skin coat to the airport, and as I wrapped and snuggled myself into it, I thought how lucky I was to have finally made it to America.

With high expectations, I went home with the mother I barely knew to meet the seven brothers and sisters who had been born in America, all of whom I had never met before.

Things went well at first, but soon my siblings became increasingly cruel to me. Naïve and unprepared, I couldn't understand why they would treat me this way. Before the year was out, I had left my parents home to strike out on my own. I may not have known anyone else in America, but I believed in myself and my self-esteem compelled my to escape the escalating cruelty of my strange siblings. With firm resolve, I decided to remove myself from all such words and behavior that seemed intended to diminish me as a person.

Within months of taking my own apartment, my home was burglarized and my passport was stolen. I determined to make it on my own, regardless of this theft, and refused to let my family know or to ask for their help. Rather, I vowed to make my American dream come true.

I attended The Barbizon Modeling School and trained to be a model, a dream I had held since high school. After graduation, I became a runway model for fashion shows in many department stores, modeled for billboard advertisements, television fashion shows, and even made it to the front page of the local newspaper as a model.

Armed with these successes, I pressed on to my second dream career of being a singer. At the time I was dating a handsome, albeit cruel, young man who showed me the newspaper one day and said, "So you think you can be a singer, well here's an advertisement for the Holiday Inn. They are looking for singers for a new Broadway show style entertainment idea. If you think you're so good, go get the job."

Commit and Go for it!

It felt exceptionally odd to enter a hotel room to meet with a stranger for an audition, but I was determined to prove myself. The person I auditioned for had an acoustic guitar and directed me to sing what I had prepared. When I was finished singing, it was immediately someone else's turn to audition. They would soon notify me of the results, they said. Low and behold, I was chosen to join the show.

Rehearsals were fun and the others chosen for the show were quite diverse. It was very exciting to rehearse all day, and then perform each night. I sang in the show titled, "The Me Nobody Knows" and "Purlie", two plays that were current big hits on Broadway.

Hooray! Another one of my American dreams had come true.

I then decided to join a rock and roll band and began auditioning for some of the locals. Again I was successful and soon began traveling all over the country singing in nightclubs, concerts and at universities. People asked me to sign autographs and I didn't understand why they wanted it, but happily signed my autograph anyway for those who asked. Eventually the band disbanded and I remembered how much I loved the city of Chicago when my band had played there.

You guessed it, I decided that Rochester, New York, was not big enough for my dreams to become a reality. I immediately rented truck, packed up all of my things, and started the long drive to Chicago.

As soon as I arrived in Chicago, I knew that I had found what I longed for in a home and I set about making some new dreams come true. I reminded myself that a dream is a goal with a deadline and pressed on.

The Dream of A Condo By the Lake
And what it took to get there

The woman had always dreamed of a condo on the lakefront of a major city. This dream seemed to be nearly impossible but she was determined, and a dreamer.

"After we were married our first apartment didn't even have furniture in it," she complained, "God, I don't even have a chair to sit in at dinnertime."

The woman's husband looked at her and explained, "If you want a condo with a view of the lake, then we can't spend a lot of money on furniture right now. We'll have to save for the condo."

After their lease was up, they decided to save even harder for their condo. So they moved to a tiny little apartment near a local "Food Town" shop. "I remember that the sound of gunshots could sometimes be heard and we would call the police and try to get them to come over—but they never showed up. Calling them was an exercise in futility. We didn't leave the house at night because the apartment was in a 'borderline' neighborhood. Actually, we never unpacked most of our belongings because we knew this was just a temporary stop on our way to our condo by the lake."

They started taking the train to work and she remembers that they had to walk through a neighborhood where there were many inconsiderate dog owners who didn't clean up after their dogs. They would have to traverse the dog remains all the way to the train station. The walk was so unpleasant that eventually they decided to take the longer bus commute to work so they could avoid this indignity.

On the bus ride there was one building that they passed daily that had a beautifully manicured and landscaped lawn in front, bordered with lovely flowers. It would always give them a warm feeling as the bus drove by it and they began thinking about the building all the time. Every day, when the bus passed the building they would say, "That's the building we're going to get our condo in." They didn't know why, they just had a feeling that this was the place.

The building wasn't extraordinarily pretty from the outside but the view of the lake at that spot was awesome, and there was a lovely harbor filled with sailboats directly across the street. Notably, there was nowhere to build in front of it, so they knew its lake views would never be obstructed.

For a year and a half they saved and saved, with their things still in storage or in boxes in their apartment. For lunch they found a place where you could get four pieces of chicken and two biscuits for five bucks. They would buy one lunch and share it, and drink water so they could save by spending no more than five dollars a day for lunch for both of them. "We 'tightened our belts' and 'pulled in our horns', forgoing dining in restaurants or taking vacations. Every penny we could spare was saved."

The day came when they finally went shopping for a condo, but no matter where they went, there was always something that didn't work out or wasn't acceptable. Naturally, they decided to investigate condos in the building they had passed while riding the bus so many times before. As though it was destined to be, everything worked out and they purchased a beautiful condo in that very building. There was only one little glitch. There was a huge burn in the middle of the carpet one of the bedrooms and the walls and ceilings were covered with pages from magazines that the previous occupant, a teenager, had left there.

Happily, they negotiated with the seller for funds to fix these two problems, but then they actually fixed the room themselves and pocketed the money. They installed new carpeting, painted the walls, installed grass cloth in the foyer and replaced all of the electrical outlets. In the end they had a beautiful condo with a view of the lake and the park, just as they had always wanted and dreamed of.

The woman in the story is me, and yes, another dream had come true.

Now sometimes when I'm around people who say, "Wow, you live on the lakefront; you're lucky." I tell them, "Thank you, it is a dream I had that became a reality because I was willing to do what it took to get there—and you can do it too. Just believe in yourself and be willing to do whatever it takes."

Some Stories of Self Creation
Maxine of Maxine's Spa—Chicago, Illinois

As a treat to myself, I get a manicure at Maxine's Spa once a week. The owner is such a young attractive woman, I observed her whenever I could. I realized that she was living a dream come true and decided to interview her for the book, so I asked her how she decided to become the owner of a Spa.

Maxine: I started with Vidal Sassoon in 1976. We started on this block and by the end of that year we had moved to Water Tower Place. I worked with Sassoon for almost 11 years and grew from shampooing hair to managing the salon. When I left in 1986 after 10 years of service, I was their Senior U.S. Manager and had trained staff that was now working in New York and LA, and it was time for me to move on. I experienced wonderful opportunities while working with that company, honed my skills, traveled around the world, and grew. But I really liked the client side of the business and I really liked the staff side of the business. However, the further up the corporate ladder I got, the further away from what really compelled me I was. Soon I decided to do my own thing.

Q: How did that come about though? Did you just get up one morning and say, "I think I'll do my own thing?"

A: Almost . . . almost. When you're reaching that time when you need to move on, sometimes you don't know it, but things aren't as smooth as they used to be. So I think I began to experience some of those same frustrations that I often find myself coaching the staff members on. One day I stepped back from myself said, "It's their ball game; it's always been the way they want to run it and why shouldn't it be? It's their company." But I respected so much about that company, I had worked there so long, obviously there was a lot there that represented a part of me. There wasn't an opportunity for me to go elsewhere because Sassoon for me was top shelf and if I was going to go anywhere else in the industry it would have had to be my own thing because to go work for another salon would not have been even a lateral move in my mind. Now, for someone else it might have been fine, but not for me.

Q: Now at that time you were a senior staff member at Sassoon, and you weren't working with clients any more?

A: I still worked with clients but the main responsibility and core of my work was managing the corporate office and building the staff, not just for Chicago, but for the other locations in the U.S., and that was where the pressure was. The pressure wasn't my client base, the pressure wasn't my staff—the pressure was corporate. I convinced myself I could do it, and I didn't necessarily feel that I wanted more of it. For me the next step would probably have been more corporate responsibilities, probably general manager, or whatever else. And I really just decided that I didn't want it. So to stay in the industry, as I said, when you work for someone else's company like that which you admire so much, to go to anywhere else on the block would not have made any sense to me. So I needed to do it my own way, and do it my own way small. And so that's what I did. But I can tell you there wasn't any great event. I decided on a weekend. It was one of those straws that breaks the camel's back.

Q: You decided over a weekend . . . .

A: Yes. I'd been toying with the idea of leaving, but not necessarily leaving to do my own thing. I was looking at design school. I was looking at going back to school, period. I was at a crossroad in my life. I was thirty-three and had roads to cross, [laughter] recently divorced and everything was up in the air. So I said, "Why not throw it all up there?"

Q: That sounds like a difficult point, though, to move in the direction of self-employment. I mean getting divorced, changing jobs. Those are both high stress situations.

A: Oh I think that the stress is getting to those points. Not doing them. The stress for me was prior to the divorce not after the divorce. The stress for me at Sassoon was prior to leaving not that I didn't, you know, create my own afterwards. But there's a tremendous sense of relief when you actually have the courage to jump.

Q: Really?

A: Personally and professionally. And then once you've done it, you're no longer trapped in the old. You're fueled by the power of new. You might be in unfamiliar territory, and it might be frightening, but nonetheless it's stimulating.

Q: So how did you get that first . . . I mean what did you do next?

A: There was a lease that was passed around Water Tower Place for some property in the neighborhood—on Walton Street, actually. And this happened probably two weeks prior to my leaving. I wasn't interested. I passed it on to a friend of mine who had a business. And within that same timeframe a couple of staff members actually came to me and they were thinking of leaving. And they said, "If ever you were to consider moving on, please consider us." I was honored; I had never ever really thought about it too much. I knew too much. I managed at a high-end national company, I knew far too much. I knew and I would always say, "I'd never do my own thing."

So anyway, a couple of management directives came down that I didn't agree with, and I couldn't bring myself to convey to the staff. And I thought, "I can't sound like the negativity that I try to coach out of people. I have to move on." So, I guess you could say that just a lot of things came together at the right time. The staff came to me, a lease was on my desk, I had taken my two weeks vacation thinking I just needed a vacation. Then I returned from vacation, but I still felt unsettled. I had worked in the same premises for 10 years by now. I was in the same mall, I came in and I did the same things, I was growing the company but it was still just a routine for me.

Q: It sounds like things were not going in the direction you would have liked.

A: Right. It was simply that I had enough information and knowledge now that I could take it and do something else with it. And I did! I went and looked at the property and gave my notice the following week. And that's what happened.

Q: And then you just went ahead and did it.

A: Well, I obviously saw a banker and had a business plan. But was I planning this for months or years in advance? No. Was owning a salon of my own ever a goal of mine? No.

Q: Were you concerned because you were single and so young and taking this bold, giant step?

A: I was more concerned with being stagnant.

Q: Which was the impetus that propelled you towards this new future?

A: Also, by now I had a new partner in my life who is still my partner in my life. The two of us thought we could make it happen, so we did.

Q: So the first location was on Walton Street.

A: Yes, and it was similar situation to this space. A small townhouse location with a walk up, but we rented and I only offered customers two services, cut and color. We were there for 5 years.

Q: How many chairs did you have when you started?

A: 12.

Q: You started with 12 chairs! So you knew even at the beginning that you would have a pretty big staff.

A: Yes maybe from your perspective. But I had just left a company with 50 chairs. So 12 was a no-brainer, and five of us were there at the start of the company and we were bringing some clients and all of us were thinking that those 5 chairs probably meant that we needed at least 10 chairs because we could easily have two people going at the same time. So that part of it wasn't so complicated.

Q: Ok, so when you moved on from Sassoon there were five of you. You and four others?

A: Yes not partners. But there were four others who came to me and they were also ready to move on. I wouldn't have had the opportunity to work with those four people anymore because, essentially, they had moved on.

Q: Would you say that that's actually indicative of your management style? That people wanted to move with you to the next location?

A: I was quite honored and I can keep a staff for a long time and I was able to do that at Vidal Sassoon, and I am able to do that for myself too.

Q: What's your method? How do you do that? Because this is not typical, though you say it so matter-of-factly, as though it's a natural skill. But not all managers have the ability to keep a staff for long periods of time.

A: I look for diamonds in the rough and I'm willing to work with someone who doesn't have any experience yet, but has the belief in themselves first and foremost, and then where the company may be taking them. When it's not right I'll be the first one to say to someone, "You know what? We need to separate." But by and large, if you spend enough time in the beginning nurturing the relationship, it can survive the challenges.

And all relationships have challenges, not just personal but professional ones. In fact I think the professional ones have more because we spend more time together.

The staff room is sometimes just like a family kitchen table, so we can really go at it. But we hire people as a company in this industry who typically do not have experience and give them the education and the experience they need to grow. In that we have the chance to buy the time to commit to one another and check out those that are not right for one another before too long a period of time has passed.

So I'm not hiring hairdressers with client bases only. I'm not buying a clientele, as I call it. I'm developing a relationship. It takes longer, but I don't have the turnover that someone else may have. I'll tell a staff member that I will do my part. I'll provide an opportunity. But your success in this industry and in this company is really based on what's inside you; not where I'm going. We talk about that a whole lot. Our industry is a hard industry, but I think most are. But everyone thinks utopia is everywhere that you're not.

Q: The grass is greener syndrome.

A: Next door may be paying a few dollars more in commission and a staff member will think that it's time to move on. And if they came to me, and I never emotionally helped grow them, then I would understand why they might consider moving. But if I can emotionally help to nurture them, then when someone comes knocking on their door they'll be less likely to hop because there's more than just a dollar commission when working here—there's a relationship. So I try to build relationships, both with staff and with clients.

Hermene Hartman, Founder of N'Digo Megapaper Interview

Q: First of all Hermene, thank you very much for sharing your weekend with me so that we could do this interview. As I said, I'm interested in how you started N'Digo, what made you create it? And what are some of the challenges you've faced that you would like to share with us about how you got from that moment when you made the decision to start the Magapaper to where you are today?

A: Well, first of all before N'digo there was a life. I was a professor in Sociology and Psychology with City Colleges of Chicago and after teaching for some years I became Director of Communications and eventually the Vice Chancellor of External Affairs. In that capacity I was responsible for marketing for the City Colleges of Chicago, its public relations and its advertising. I built a Communications Department that started out with one person and ended up with a department of 12.

We were a full fledged marketing and communications department with Public Relations, Marketing and Printing, Imaging and so forth at the College. In that capacity, when I started the marketing and advertising for students I realized how limited the print media market was in the City of Chicago for both the students who attended the college and me.

That thought stayed in my mind for a couple of years. The other thing was, while I had done public relations before, I had worked with CBS as a producer for TV, the outlet for black intelligence was not in the media and I was very frustrated by that.

You know, you can see "shake your booty", you can see "bang, bang shoot them up", you could see the scandals, and you the media can supply the negative stereotype so very much; but what you don't see is what I consider really to be a norm: the black doctor, you don't see the black lawyer, you don't see the black business person, you don't see the college student.

So the black middle class, as I see it, was absent from the media. I mean they were very underserved, very misunderstood, very misrepresented. You would only see what I call the superstars, the super story, either the super poor, "Here's a woman with 10 kids and the children eat out of a garbage can"; or you see Michael Jordan's every movement, you see Oprah Winfrey's every movement, but there's more people in the middle.

There are people who go to work, people who pay taxes, people who join the workforce, people who send their children to college, that element was missing, and so that was my focus. That became my focus. I kept asking myself, "Where is that person?" The other thing I noticed is what I call "beyond Black History Month". You see so much African American whatever during Black History Month, but you really see a recycling of the same things. The same heroes, the same instances, the same historical events. Meanwhile contemporary culture is lost, it's ignored, it's again misunderstood.

When Harold Washington was Mayor of Chicago, I guess that's when it really became glaringly obvious. Who is Harold Washington? Where did Harold Washington come from? What is Harold Washington talking about? Things got to the point where some of the responses were almost silly and insulting.

I remember Walter Jacobson the day that Harold was inaugurated; Walter Jacobson and Harry Porterfield were the anchors and "Lift Every Voice", the National Black Anthem was sung at the inauguration and Jacobson turned to Porterfield to say "Oh, is this a new song? Or is this a song that was created for this special occasion?" And Porterfield said, "No, this is not a new song," and gave a history of the song, explaining that it was the National Negro Anthem and Jacobson said, "I didn't know that there was a National Negro Anthem."

Now that's an incident. To me that is why there's a lot of cultural ignorance, just downright ignorance. And I thought that it was time for, immediate crossover media. Crossover in that just as we read the Tribune, Caucasians could read N'Digo, but there needed to be a print medium for U.S. African Americana about U.S. addressing contemporary issues, contemporary people and personalities, and I have three principles that I use. I wanted to do it with style, I wanted to do it with sense and I wanted to do it with substance.

That was the genesis, the thinking; that was the intelligence of N'Digo, and why N'Digo and what my original thought, my original thinking was for creating N'Digo.

Q: So did you sit down and write a business plan then?

A: I became ill and I'd never been sick before. I was home for about 6 weeks. So the thought, the idea, had been in my mind, but the reality actually happened while I was sick. I am a pretty high-energy person so lying in bed was not my cup of tea at all. Anyway, that became my work and every day for about 4 hours I would spend some concentrated time on developing the idea.

I did not do the business plan first; I did the paper. I laid out the look, I laid out the content, I laid out the editorial, as to what it would be, what it would look like, what stories it would cover, what things one would do in it. I laid all of that out first and designed it. Then I came back with the business plan.

I began to talk to some friends, and one friend, Paul King, who's a businessperson, said, "Now you've got to move beyond the creative concepts into business. This will be a business for you, not a hobby, not a creative venture, so you've got to merge business into it." So I went to my accountant and we started doing the business plan and I hired a guy whose area of expertise was writing business plans—some of the most difficult sessions I have ever been in, but he made you think it through.

You know: Where's your money coming from? How will you pay for this? Where's your advertising coming from? How will you make business out of this? Those were very, very wonderful and good sessions because it was the structure of the business.

The other thing that I did is I wanted to test N'Digo. I wanted to test the concepts; I wanted to test the business. I went to the Sun Times and I said to them, "You all do an awful black business month section. It's almost insulting what you do." But I told them it was just not good, which it wasn't, and I pointed out the what and the why. Then I said, "Would you let me do a black history month special for you? They said, "OK, fine."

They sold the advertising and I did the editorial content. What I was really doing is market testing. We did a full run in the paper in February and it was overwhelmingly successful. One, it crossed over and I wanted to see if it had that capability, and two, I wanted to see what the audience reception would be, and three, and this was a sign that it actually worked, people began to call and ask for it by itself. "We would like that section," [they'd say,] and the Sun Times were charging $3.00 for it.

So I thought Aha, there is a revenue stream. We can do this.

Q: What was the demographic of the people who responded? Were they the people you wanted?

A: Yes, they were my target audience: black middle-class and white progressives. The exact people I wanted. It worked very well, and it was only eight pages.

Q: Did you find then that as this readership started requesting it that you were learning about black middle class or black business people that were not on your radar screen previously?

A: Not really, that's who I wanted—that was my demographics.

Q: I mean like a company, for example.

A: Oh yes, but it didn't happen until later on. That was the prototype and then after about a year that's when we really started the paper. N'Digo's first publication was December of '89 and we took the elements of what we learned and other elements of what I wanted: style, fashion, food, the cover was magazine like, Vogue-ish, with pretty pictures on the cover.

I went to Europe. I was like a maniac. I was just studying, looking at papers, watching what people picked up. I came back from Europe with the idea of doing oversize. In Europe the papers are oversized—they're a bit larger than our papers—so I developed a paper that was just a little bit oversized because I was trying to enter the marketplace with a uniqueness; with a difference and so the oversize, I thought, would capture the audience.

I had studied how people picked up papers, free papers in particular, and I thought the picture needed to be captivating so that you would gravitate to it and that was very successful. Those were some of the things that we learned.

We did a lot of market research after N'Digo came out for about a year. It was a very high learning curve. We asked people why they picked it up, what they liked, what they enjoyed, what they didn't like, what they wanted to leave out. So at that time, the people that you talked about, maybe new businesses or people just about doing things, that's when we began to find those people and companies, and where those people are and what they do and so forth.

We were monthly at first, and then we went bi-weekly and then we went weekly. After our first year we became an insert in the Sun Times. We were an insert in the Sun Times for about 18 months. As I became a more sophisticated publisher, I realized that this oversized paper was costing me more money and so we trimmed it down to a new size and the cover became color. Our first issues were black and white.

Q: Was there a lot of pain in the beginning and how did you deal with that?

A: When you say "pain," what do you mean?

Q: I mean, as part of the learning curve getting started. Are you working out of your home, working over the telephone with people because you're working from home, or do you open an office immediately?

A: I wouldn't call it pain, it was more growth. It's hard work. I worked out of my home with a P.O. Box number for all of maybe three months. Then my mother said to me, "You need to get out of this house. This house is not an office." She just said, "You need an office."

So, my first office was at 54 West Hubbard and it was a large co-operative office. They were political consultants. I was still teaching for the first three years of N'Digo. I worked and did not take a salary out of it, and I worked out of that office for awhile.

Q: I assume that there are maybe three of you? At what point did that happen?

A: No. I had a meeting with some friends who were writers, photographers and graphic artists, who were very good. I said to them, "We're going to do a paper and I need all of you to help and we're going to showcase our skills—our profession." They needed to work in their profession. They all had the skills and all qualified for mainstream media, but for whatever reason they were not working for them.

So, I suggested that we work for ourselves. We would create a paper called N'Digo and we would do the same thing mainstream media does, and I said, "Don't talk to me for one year about money because there is none. Let's just do it and then after a year we will have a viable business. This is an experiment. This is a 'let's see if it will work.'" And everybody rolled up their sleeves, and that was kind of the attitude for the first year.

I think maybe the story you are thinking of is that I went to a banker for money for the paper and my loan was turned down. Media property is one of the most difficult businesses to get funding for because they are abstractions. They are not concrete there is no brick and mortar, there's no building to come for. You are selling creativity and advertising and that works or doesn't work, but the banker cannot get collateral from it.

So I was rejected; I was turned down. I thought that I would be eligible for SBA money from the Federal Government and had that in the back of my mind—that that would be a funding source. However, at that time SBA funded everything but media—that was an exception and something they didn't fund. Because if the government gave you money then would you be biased towards the government in your reporting, was the thinking.

So I didn't have any money and I didn't get any money from any outside sources. I am a bootstrap operation. My money came from advertisers, and what I did in my early days was, I told advertisers that they had to pay up front. I had a policy called "place and take": you place the ad and you pay for the ad at the same time—the same transaction—and that was unheard of, but it worked for me.

Q: Do you still use the "place and take" method?

A: I'm beginning to use it more and more with this economy being what it is today. Yes, I am using it a lot right now. And I would say with your larger companies, with your larger companies that is a hard policy to implement because they don't typically work like that. They work 30 days to 60 days out. So for the larger companies we do bill, but for the smaller companies, indeed, I have some companies that just must pay up front. They must provide payment in advance. You weed out a lot of bad guys that way.

Q: I'm sure you do. Now what was your circulation when you started?

A: 50,000. It started off at 50,000.

Q: And what is it now?

A: Current circulation is 125,000

Q: Now at 50,000, when you started, what measures did you use to determine if the paper was indeed being read? My understanding is that for print media, at the end of the month or week or whatever the distribution is, the publisher comes in and picks up the remaining papers.

A: That's exactly how it works, and your distribution department, whatever the timeframe of your paper is, you pick up the old and you put in the new. Well, we never had too many pick ups. We didn't have returns. They were gone. So the market was hungry for it.

The first issue of N'Digo flew off the shelves. These were indicators that told me that we could have this paper every week. So that was part of the vision. We were always working towards getting it to a weekly issue.

Q: Did you have partners?

A: No. I started off with a partner. I had done all the planning, and had the printing and had the writers and this, that, and the other—but one thing I forgot was the truck to deliver the paper. And so I brought in a partner. I had helped him in another business enterprise and he said, "Well, I'll take care of the truck." So that gave him about 20% of the business. We eventually parted ways after about the first year.

Q: Do you have partners today?

A: No. I own 100% of the company.

Q: At what point did you realize that you could transition and devote 100% of your time to N'Digo with a full staff?

A: Well, we functioned for about 3 years in this one office and used a lot of freelancers for writers. I paid for the writers. Then we participated in an expo; the Chicago Tribune kept coming to our booth to pick up papers. I was not at the booth at the time, but my partner told me, "The Tribune keeps coming over here and taking the papers." And I asked, "Well? What are they saying?" And he said, "Nothing, they're just picking up the paper." So I said, "Where's their booth?"

When I found their booth I went over and introduced myself and I said, "I understand you're picking up our papers. Would you please tell me why?" A young lady said, "Well, we might have an interest in your paper. Would you come in and talk to us?" So we talked with the Tribune, and after three years we formed a strategic alliance with the Tribune. What that meant was that they gave us funding to expand so that we could have a staff.

They printed the paper, and most importantly they gave mentoring from the very top level of the company. They mentored me into being a publisher. The Tribune has training and they allowed our people to be trained under their auspices and classes with their own employees. So what they really provided is, they opened up and allowed us to learn from what I consider to be one of the biggest and best newspaper companies in Chicago and the newspaper business.

So that is where I really, really began. I was learning small business, business operations, business procedures, and so on and so forth. But it's the Tribune that said, "Let us teach you the business of publishing. You need to go into newspaper publishing." So they mentored me, and I'm to this day elated, because N'Digo would not nearly be where it is today had that not happened.

Q: That's wonderful. They shared their knowledge and resources with you.

A: Yes, and that is really great. Personnel, analysis, just opened up a big company to a little company and that was really valuable.

Q: Now at this time, did you have N'Digo in those boxes that we see now on the street corner?

A: That came from the Tribune experience: you've got to put some papers there. The best place for a paper is inside an organization, inside a building, inside a church, inside a school. Inside is your best place, but not every place is going to let you in. So your second best place is in a box outside your transportation lines, for example. That's where most papers are sold.

Even for large publishers like the Tribune and the Sun Times, half of their papers are sold like that on the street. So we very strategically began to place our boxes. We opened up downtown. Paper boxes are very expensive so we were very strategic about where we placed our boxes. Again, that was a Tribune innovation employed by us.

Q: So did the papers fly out of the boxes just as they had before?

A: It was very well received.

Q: Did the association with the Tribune, then, give you the opportunity to say, add the paper as inserts into their Sunday issue?

A: No, we did not insert. That was something we discussed; because I designed N'Digo in its original format to be an insert into major newspapers and the reason is I thought it would help them with their diversity coverage.

A lot of major media don't cover Blacks or Hispanics because they don't have the sensitivity to do it. If they do attempt it, they usually do it poorly and they do it poorly because of a lot of ignorance, a lot of stereotypes. There's a lot of stupidity and a lot of "We don't really know what's important," and so I thought an N'Digo type product would benefit them. You see, the cities have changed, the demographics have changed and they need to do something to cover it.

What a lot of these institutions do when they hire a Hispanic or Black reporter is, they don't hire them to be Black and Hispanic. They eventually carve them to be the duplicate of what they are. So they hire you for that, but then they make you into themselves, so you still lose the identity. You still lose the focal point of what you're trying to do. So I thought that N'Digo would be its own flavor and an independent perspective.

But, every newspaper has to have a voice. Every medium has a voice and N'Digo inside the Tribune might still become the Tribune voice. This was a big question, but we thought it through.

Jack Fuller, who is now over all of the newspapers of the Tribune, is a very good friend. I just adore him; we had serious discussions on the meaning of a newspaper. What is the editorial of a newspaper supposed to do? A newspaper is supposed to be a voice and that is what I wanted it to be: "a voice" not a supplement, not an advertising adjunct, but a voice, and to be a voice, you have to be independent.

So the example that I use, because I brought this up, is if there was a conflict, if there was a problem I wanted it on the table in front.

So how do we solve this so this is a win-win for both of us? An example that I use is Harold Washington when he was running for Mayor, and if you remember, no major newspaper endorsed Harold Washington. That was a real indication to me—that was my interpretation—of how out of touch these newspapers were with their readers.

That was one interpretation, my interpretation, because anybody walking into Chicago knew that Harold Washington was going to win. It was a ground swell, and you could feel that. However, Harold Washington was not endorsed by a single major media in the Chicago area. That being the example, if Harold Washington was running today, I would endorse him, and how would you feel about that? And the answer was, "Yes, we would."

Q: I'm surprised. But at least they were honest enough about how they felt.

A: Well, that was been there, done that. It was, if you remember, Byrne, Daley and Washington and they endorsed, was that a white black issue? If I didn't endorse Harold Washington, my readership would say, "What the hell are you doing here?" So that was the example that we used and I would have written an editorial and I would have endorsed him, and they said they would have problems with that. So, to be an independent voice, you've got to be just that.

So what would you do if N'Digo endorsed Harold Washington inside the Tribune as a supplement, and the Tribune endorses someone else? Are we confusing readers here, are we giving readers diversity, are we giving readers choices or are we conflicting what scenarios we look at? So we very consciously decided that those types of incidents could come up conservative versus liberal, progressiveness, black versus white, big versus small. There were a lot of elements there where we could absolutely be on the opposite side of the fence.

Ultimately we decided we would *be* an independent voice, and Jack Fuller helped to think that through in a very intellectual discussion on "What is a Newspaper?" And, it was at his urging, he said, "You've got to be a voice, to follow your mission and to do what you want."

Q: So did you have a mission and a vision statement at that time?

A: Yes. To be a voice. Absolutely, because there is no black voice out there.

Q: Do you think that's still true?

A: I think we've become the voice.

Q: Exactly . . . and you're the only voice.

A: I wish some more folks would jump in, but yes, we've become the voice.

Q: How did you decide, especially as a weekly newspaper, with such a short turn around time, what your issue will be from week to week?

A: The editor and I sit down and plan 8 to 10 weeks out. The columnists write their own [material]; we don't tell them what to write. They are their own conscience. I write a column and it is a contemporary social commentary, and I make that decision. Do I sit down and plan? I will do some generic things I would like to write for each issue. You know, things change so fast and you are reacting and responding to the current events of the day and there's only so much planning that you can really do with that.

There might be a book out. I might write about the book so that's a planned writing and I'm a planner. I do like to plan, so I call those sheet columns, when there's a book I might write about. But we pretty much from week to week we try to look at maybe the time of year, Dr. King's birthday, or maybe Black History month, those become global statement type columns.

That's pretty much how we do it. We look at the news, what's going on; we look at contemporary issues and write in response to that or politics that might be going on.

Q: Did you concentrate on Chicago or did you go to the outlying areas like Peoria, or other areas? Because I believe that you're in more markets now.

A: We're Chicagoland. Our paper is distributed from Evanston [Illinois] to Gary, Indiana. We're not in Peoria; we're not in Illinois, we're in Chicagoland. Evanston North, because we got requests for N'Digo there and Gary, Indiana, South because we got requests for it there in the South suburbs, not in great numbers but we're there.

Q: Have you expanded outside to places like Washington, DC?

A: No.

Q: Is that a planned strategy? And why did you decide not to go beyond Chicagoland?

A: We made that decision because N'Digo is a local newspaper and when you start going outside of the local area that would change it. For it to be appealing in Washington, it would have to be a national newspaper—it's got to be a Newsweek, it's got to be a Wall Street Journal type, and that's not what it is. It is a local newspaper. We have a magazine called *N'Digo Profiles* that lends itself better to a national audience than N'Digo as a newspaper does.

Q: Tell me about the magazine.

A: *N'Digo Profiles* is an annual edition of N'Digo that we do. It has a theme. We've done 7 issues so far, we are approaching our 8th issue, but we've themed, each issue: men, women, couples, entertainers, entrepreneurs, and then we've done two.

The fist one was just a spectrum a composite of people, and then the seventh one was just a spectrum from the millennium of what we've done. We have profiled people within the spectrum of their respective disciplines and fields. So that lends itself nationally, and we do have our eye on that becoming national because you see, it won't have local news, it will have maybe local people but all the people will be world class global types.

Q: I noticed that you have a website now. When did you start that and why? And how is it going?

A: Well, the website is the way of the marketplace, so just to keep up with the market we established the website. It is not as fully developed as I want it to be, with all the bells and whistles, but we're working on it right now to develop it a lot better. Right now it is just the content of the paper, but I would like to develop it into a portal where we would sell unique things on it and talk about events and activities. It's at this initial stage, but it needs a web master's mind to develop it.

When the dot-com craze came we got in it and when they went I thought we'd better leave this alone for a minute and concentrate on our core business of what we really do, which is print. Then we can come back to it later and we'll do the presentation plan the communications plan, but its not fully developed yet. It's still a work in progress.

Q: How have you changed since starting? I have a great understanding of where you got the "aha" moment—where you said this is an area that needs attention. How have you changed as a person? Has it changed you as a person?

A: I should hope I've developed and honed my business skills. One of the most important things in business is making decisions—your whole decision making process. I hope I'm a better decision maker than I was on day one, and what every employer must do to develop an organization is develop human capital. That's the most important thing you can do: to take people and develop them.

To see where people are, to see where they fit into your organization, to see where they grow, to see how to develop them, and in the process of doing that, to see what they contribute to your organization and to your business. I hope I can do that a lot better. That's been growth for me.

Managing money, making the right decisions . . . what I try to do every year, I work on adding new elements doing something different, doing something better. Media is a changing, quick-moving kind of business, and every year I add, I change, we do something different and those are calculated moves. Because where the good moves are progression, make the wrong move and you can shoot yourself in the foot, too.

At one point, if I was invited to speak or invited to do this, or to do that, when N'Digo was very young and was working on getting a name out—getting the brand out—getting the product out—I would attend mostly everything. I don't do that so much anymore. I'm much more decisive and much more strategic in what I do personally, where I go, and what I lend my name to. Because now my participation takes on another meaning.

My time is very important to me. You caught me this morning, this is the first time in maybe five years when I got up late. I was just bone tired. I'm beginning to guard my time, my energy. People come to you with so much stuff and there's a real appreciation for friends for the sake of you not for the sake of them or for the sake of their project or for the sake of whatever it is for the moment.

Being able to decipher that has been hard. I'm divorced. I'm not married. I used to get these calls that's so interesting. These guys would call [saying], "I'd like to take you to dinner, I'd like to take you for lunch, I'd like to do this, I'd like to do that," and ultimately, they're talking about "Put me on the cover of the paper. Let me tell you about my business." So now I say, "Tell me what you want. You don't need to take me to dinner to give me your press release." I don't need to go to dinner for that, I'd be 500 pounds if I did that. So those are just some of the things related to my growth.

Q: Are you involved at all in the political arena? Do you attend the events?

A: [Laughing] By the nature of the business of what I do, it is inevitable. But I pick and choose; I don't attend all of them. Because you have to give fair coverage, you always have to be balanced in your coverage and we have to cover it correctly. We do have a political editor so it's not a Hermene decision.

We sit down and talk, and we say we should support this one because of that. So we work it out in an amenable, editorial way. If I do have a candidate that I like I try to separate the personal support from the business editorial support. You know what I mean.

Q: Yes. And as you mention that I am reminded of something that I read recently in N'Digo, and as I read it I thought, "I wonder how she deals with this sort of verbal attack?" You wrote a column about a professor who did a hip-hop CD, and I'll commend you on this: I read it in N'Digo first and then I saw it on *The O'Reilly Factor*, and I thought it was very interesting because I already had that juxtaposition of your remarks in your column and the response to your column.

A: And everybody wrote, because after that it looked like we really stepped out there first—after that, the New York Times, Wall Street Journal—just whoosh! Everybody began to write about it and it's become quite a discussion.

Q: It's pretty high on the radar screen for everybody right now.

A: Yes.

Q: How do you feel when you get responses from your readership that are critical of your views? Where they are less interested, it seems to me, in your objectives for writing this column than they are in their agenda of why you shouldn't have taken that position?

A: Well, first of all N'Digo becomes a forum. A columnist writes opinionated pieces; that's what a columnist does. And I write social commentary and my opinions. Everybody is not going to agree with you. It's not for agreement

Robert Blackwell of Blackwell Consulting INTERVIEW

Q: I appreciate your accepting this interview and giving me of your time so that I can share with the readers of the book how you self created. This book Self Creation: 10 Powerful Principles for Changing Your Life, is all about taking control of your future and your own destiny. I think you did that when you started your consulting firm.

A: Well you know, when you talk about self creation on one level, it wasn't self creation. I've been blessed by several things. One, I had wonderful parents which wasn't due to anything that I did, who raised me in a nurturing home. I was fortunate to have athletic ability, which got me into college, I was fortunate to have a wonderful wife who in my dark days when I was young and struggling to get meaning, was just insistent that I could be somebody. Then I went on and studied and I worked at IBM and IBM provided me a platform where I could develop skills in the computer business. They also gave me the wherewithal to learn how to sell computers and how to deal. So I learned an awful lot of my professional skills working for IBM company.

What I would give myself credit for is that after 25 years at IBM and deciding to go out on my own, I do have a good sense of self. I have a good sense of myself. I am comfortable with who I am and I am comfortable that I have the ability to do what I put my mind to, and so I am not a naysayer. I wake up every day thinking to myself, what am I going to do today. I'm not worried about the problems I had yesterday, except in so far as what can I change or what can I do different. But I don't second guess my ability to compete effectively in the marketplace. This is a message I so often give to African

Americans that they've got to get over this idea that we cannot perform, that we can't effectively compete. Everything we touch, we do well and we just have to make up our minds to do that.

Q: What made you start your own company?

A: My son nagging me. I happen to have a son who is a real entrepreneur who kept pushing me and saying "you ought to go into business for yourself. You should do it, its easier, you will make more money. I am the counter example of the father passing the torch to the son. In my case it was the son passing the torch to the father and teaching me and encouraging me to get into business. That's how I got into business which is an interesting story.

I was kind of a one company guy, sitting there happy growing through the company and my son kept saying, "you know you're kind of crazy." So my son had the company first. And that's what I mean, you have to be careful about the notion of self creation because all along the road you have people that are supportive. The problem is, there's an old saying that somebody can teach you something, but they can't learn for you." Because I've had a lot of help but I just reached a point where I think that my mind is ready to learn and to adapt and to do those things. I do think it's an interesting twist that a 55 year old guy became an entrepreneur through the pushing and encouraging of his son which is kind of a nice story.

Q: So you started your company at 55?

A: Yes, I did and that was 10 years ago. Actually the fact is, I've got my Medicare, Blue Cross part A and B in my pocket.

Q: How long did it take to really get the company off the ground, to really get that first customer, that big contract to get you going?

A: had it when I walked out the door. I thought carefully about leaving. I planned carefully, and my strength is sales, and I know you can't do a job unless you get a job, so when I walked out I had a job. I had a job with IBM they were nice enough to do that and so they were my first customer. So in terms of financial viability, I think from the very day that we started we were a real business doing real things. I think though that like a lot of businesses we've hit a plateau point and I think we are now in a position that with a little luck, a lot of talent and hard work that we're positioned to be a solid mid-sized business as opposed to a small business. And so what you're always trying to do is move to different levels so that you continually drive yourself up the chain. So in that sense, you always feel unsuccessful, you know, you always feel like "yeah, I'm good but I'm 27 Million, IBM is 100 Billion, there's a long ways to go.

Q: Wouldn't you say though that that's more of a great motivator and a reason to not become complacent?

A: That's right, that's where I am, not to become complacent. Not to rest on your laurels to wake up everyday trying to drive your company forward and do everything you can to provide value. Yes, I do agree. See, now when people tell me that I have a really good company, I take that and I appreciate the compliment and on the positive side, my chest sticks out a little bit. But then, that's not what drives you ahead. What you have to do is to look in front of you and see all those people in front of you and make up your mind that this time next year, I'm going to pass some of them. Not all of them, but a few.

Q: So what I think I just heard you say is that although some people consider you and your company a success, you still have goals to best the competition, grow bigger, go global?

A: Yes, all of the above.

Q: Do you really look at other companies as the competition?

A: Yes, and sometimes you do it in an admiring way. You look at firms and you think "how do I stack up against these firms? What do they really do? Why are they beating me? How can I compete more effectively?"

Q: So what do you think is the secret of your success?

A: Getting up every morning, going back. You know, everybody says this, and very few people believe it. It's just determination, persistence.

Q: Were you ever discouraged?

A: Yes, discouraged all the time, but you just get up and be persistent. You know, because everyday something good happens, everyday something bad happens. At the end of the day, its 10 to 8 in the favor of the good things. It's never 10 to 0. There's always problems, there's always something that goes wrong. But it's important at the end of the day, and here I'm a bit religious, you have to thank God for all the good things that happened and thank God for all the bad things that happened. Because in the aggregate, you learn from the bad things and you don't do them again; and you learn from the good things and you try to repeat those things and then you move on. But if you think that you're going to be in business and a portion of your success is that you don't have a lot of failure, forget it, you're going to fail.

Q: Did you tap into the African American market to help your company be more successful?

A: Well it depends on how you say that. I don't have any African American customers per se, except for a few. And there are some notable ones. There is a lady who is an investment manager, who gave me one of my first jobs and was always so kind to me. She helped me when I was really small and I have always been very appreciative of that. But in the main I do business with large Fortune 500 companies and large universities. But in your question, there is another question. What is the relationship of a black owned African American firm who doesn't have any black clients and then what should the relationship be to the African American community? The answer of course is that every African American community, every African American company is totally dependent upon their success in the African American constituency. If I'm making sense to you. African American companies rest on how African Americans are doing. If African Americans are doing well, I'm going to be doing well. If somebody decides that African Americans are not going to do well, I am not going to do well. So if the politicians decide they are going to create a less attractive environment for black businesses I'm going to get hurt. If politicians create a more favorable environment for African Americans, I'm going to be impressed. Right? If the African American community stands up and pushes and drives in support of business, I benefit. So I know that I am inextricably linked to my people. Are you with me? Regardless of where the specific revenues come from into my company. So therefore, as a business I put money back into the black community. I come to BDPA, I come to ITSMF, and it is not charity, it's business. Because African American companies cannot separate themselves the overall welfare of their people. You know, they just can't and be successful.

Q: If I recall correctly, I read somewhere that your company has a very diverse cultural environment. Did you specifically design it that way?

A: Yes I did.

Q: Why?

A: Because I believe it's better. I've had wonderful experiences hiring women. When I was at IBM I began to hire women. You know it is funny what you do in adversity. I had a branch office on the far south side of Chicago in Calumet City servicing steel. And a lot of really bright young white fellows and bright young black fellows didn't want to go down to this little kind of ugly branch handling these dying industries. So I said "fine you guys don't have to come. I went over and started hiring women. Now, because a lot of people weren't hiring women in those days I had the most talented women you've ever seen. I had the cream of the crop and they came down to this branch and I saw what an enormous difference these women made. At one time I had 13 to 15 managers who were women and I saw all the opposition to them. You see people might not talk to me about what they thought about being black, but guys will talk to me about what they don't like about women. And so all the things about being pregnant and all that stuff. So I have had great experience with hiring and working with women.

The second thing that I thought which I knew because I had been in the business, is that the technical business is a global business. People all over the world know this stuff. And it's empirical in the sense that it's a matter of brain power, its not experience. Its like mathematics and music, the geniuses are always real young and they come to it. Computers are like that, young people understand this stuff. So what I wanted to do and here African American businesses make a mistake if they don't take their own equality measures seriously. The answer is I'm hiring people who know how to do the work for our customers. If they're from India, if they are from South Africa, and I'm naming companies where we're doing business, Russia, Ireland, hey, we're hiring them, white, black, blue, green, we are going to put together a combination of people who provide superior work for our clients. Now, what's really important here is that this diversity include African Americans and that we get over this notion that somehow African Americans are a breed of people who are the only people on earth who can't understand computers.

Q: I never heard that.

A: Well, I'll tell you something, if you go around the world and you go to South Africa or Ireland, or India or the Philippines and all those populations where they have homogeneous populations [not South Africa obviously] you can find incredibly talented people in large numbers. My experience is, the hardest place to find technical people in large numbers is here in the U.S. amongst African Americans. It's difficult because for whatever reasons, and you can go through the slavery argument or whatever, mathematics, science, tough subjects, hard courses are things that we have been discouraged from over the years. We've had people tell us not to do that and it's had an impact. But I'm here to say that African Americans can do this business and so they have to be in this mix of diversity. You see, African Americans always do well when they get opportunities. So that's my diversity thing.

Q: That's highly commendable, and I completely agree with you.

A: But you cant just say, look, what I'm going to do is I'm going to build a business and I'm going to hire just African Americans. Because then my question would be, "well what is the problem you're trying to solve, what's this guy trying to do. This person you just hired, this African American is going to have to do this. Now if he doesn't know how to do this, it's not a matter of what he doesn't know. The answer is that client's not paying you for people who can't do the work. It's our job to get this person to the point where they can do the work.

Q: So what do you do in that case, do you train them? Do you release them from their contract with the company?

A: Well my thinking is that's one of the reasons why you belong to organizations like Black Data Processing Associates (BDPA), it's very difficult for a firm like mine to hire people who don't know and don't understand how to do the work. So we almost always have to hire experienced people in our firm. Giant firms have enormous training budgets and the like. So then what I try to do is to feel a sense of responsibility of dealing with people who are responsible for developing these talents and encouraging them and supporting them. BDPA, DePaul University, I do some work with DeVry, I do work with Robert Morris, I'm invested in global Chicago many other efforts to get technology literacy and competence in. That is my business motive for why I'm with BDPA and more importantly why I do some work with young people in the elementary schools and middle schools so that we can get these kids coming forward.

And in fact in the computer business, computer skills is not the most important skill. The most important skill is analytical skill, intelligence, a broad based education and the ability to think. So the fact that someone knows a computer language C++ and they can't speak very well, they cant speak very well, can't write very well, don't have good analytical skills, don't think clearly, the computer skill is a total waste.

Q: So I guess you're saying that in order to be success you need to have good business sense and an education. Do you have a Masters Degree?

A: No, I don't. I graduated from college but that was it. You see, I am blessed. Here's another place where I am blessed. When I came along computers were just coming on the scene. 19666, there were not computer schools. So, IBM which was the dominant computer company in the world at the time, trained me. They had their own school and they taught me everything I ever needed to know about computers. So the question is, do I fell like I have a graduate degree given what I did and the answer is, I learned from a company that is the best in the business so the answer is yes.

Q: Do you think that you have to have a Masters Degree in order to really make it in today's business world?

A: No, I don't. I don't believe it at all. I think that all the education you can have is helpful. But please remember that Bill Gates did not graduate from college. Now, that does not say that Bill Gates is not an extremely intelligent well-educated man. And here I don't want to get degrees mixed up. For example, I do believe that business school going to business school has enormous advantage. That doesn't mean that if you don't go to business school that you can't run a business obviously. But you've got to learn it somewhere and my feeling is that educational institutions shortcut the process.

Q: Did you start the process by writing a business plan using that time proven step and process when you started the company?

A: Yes I did. In fact we developed and very carefully planned using something called the MIT plan. You go research these various business plans at the library or at Borders book store and there's all these commercial business plans. Some of them are crappy commercial things but MIT had developed a process whereby they thought that it was an effective way to put together a business plan. I liked their approach and so we used their approach. And of course, we tweak it and change it all the time. The purpose of a business plan is not so much to last forever, but it is a pointer and a guide to where you want to be. And then as you go along you need to reassess all the time how you're doing. But it's very difficult to figure out where you are if you don't know where you're going. So the business plan is important.

Q: As we were heading here to do this interview you ran into someone from your past and it was an very warm experience as I kind of saw you transcend time and be touched by someone you helped so many years ago. Does this happen to you often?

A: Yes it does. And please know that doesn't because I'm unusual, it happens because I'm getting old. You know the fact of the matter is that I'm the same person that I was when I was 30, 28 years old and I was there in the 60s when there were all the race riots and the civil rights stuff that was going on and people have to choose what they're going to do with their lives and how they're going to approach it. I thought then what I think now, you have to help the upcoming generation to be better. My view of a parent is that if your child is not better than you are, then you didn't do a very good job. You child ought to know more than you, be smarter than you because they took everything you knew plus added to it. So what you see in this case is a young guy who was the beneficiary of a six week computer program that I ran, oh God, that was 1969, 1970. I do know that I was 30 years old then and everyone was talking about how black kids couldn't do this and black kids couldn't do that and I knew that that was crap.

So I convinced IBM to let me take the summer off and run a computer class, OK and they told me I could run the computer class, but I couldn't take the summer off. So I said OK and I got my clients to agree. Now at that time my main client was St. Francis Hospital with a very modern computer facility that they agreed to let us use the computers in the evening. You know I ran a completely tough program with 12 kids and we had jobs all lined up for them when they came to work in the class. We committed to the firms that they would have qualified workers when they were released from the program and anybody who didn't finish the program or didn't do very well we cold cut them. I committed and we had 12 jobs and 12 kids and those kids knew that those jobs were waiting for them. It was an incentive, and then I worked them like dogs and didn't put up with any crap and I had high expectations and I told them that you're going to do this work right and you're not going to miss a step. And don't you dare tell me anything about being black you cant do that and those kids all got jobs and they all did well and a couple of them made computers their life's work like Keith Gardner who you just met.

Q: Excellent. Now, this is my second time speaking at the BDPA conference but this is the first time I heard about ITSMF. Someone said you started that or have something to do with that. Can you tell me what that is?

A: Yes. First of all, I did not start it. It is the Information Technology Senior Management Forum. It is a group of people who are senior level IT executives in large organizations who are African American who came together in a bonding and a way to share their common problems and their common interests to deal with the issues that African Americans run into. I believe that there is a gentleman who came into Amoco who is now the Senior Vice President and CIO at the Principal Group named Carl Williams who started it. I have belonged to it for a couple of years and its nice. My motivation for it is that it is kind of a reprieve. You know sometimes you need to kind of take a step back and relax and talk to people in kind of a protected way about the problems you run into who understand what you're talking about. So that is ITSMF and so they then have a link to BDPA and they provide BDPA with some senior level management advise and organizational skills that kind of thing.

Q: Recently I saw the Fortune 50, a list of African Americans who hold senior level positions and I imagine that ITSMF is something like that.

A: Yes, it is.

Q: My objective here is to have people in the book who made a decision to change their life, executed on that decision and then were successful in their chosen objective. Did you have people who stepped forward and helped you to get started; people who said "I believe in you" and helped you in that regard?

I always felt IBM was really supportive, my family was really supportive and I had some people who left IBM with me who were very, very supportive and so, yeah I would say I was supported. I would also say though that much of running a business is a solitary business.

Q: Still?

A: Yes. I mean all kinds of people help you and you couldn't function without them but it's also true, at least in my case that a lot of managing a business is a solitary exercise where you have to think about your business and dream about it, and eat it and just chew it. I mean, we're sitting in a place now called Walt Disney, right? When I was a young person, none of this existed. Walt Disney was an animator for God's sake and an illustrator. He used to win all the academy awards for animation every year and you can just imagine that he had this driving ambition that was propelling him and so in that sense I think that business from the founder and chief executive's point of view to be a solitary endeavor. Right? But having said that, nobody is an island and it doesn't get a lot of support a lot of help a lot of assistance. I have debts to people that have helped me that would go from here to China. But on the other side of that, if you decide that you are going to run a business, you have to be really committed to it. And you really do, I like the word eat it because it becomes in you and part of you and not separable from you. And if you don't do that, then probably your business will never achieve quite what you would want it to.

Q: Do you have a coach, or a mentor? I mean, today, now.

A: Well that's an interesting question and the answer is yes. The answer is that for 10 years he wouldn't say that he was a mentor but for 10 years I have sat down with a guy that I have enormous respect for and every three months we have lunch together, a long 2-hour lunch and we talk about my business. And I tell him what I'm doing, I tell him what I'm thinking about and he tells me what he thinks and he gives me advice. He is an African American that nobody knows. He is a brilliant guy who was a CEO of his own firm, was once featured in Fortune Magazine as probably the first black man who was going to be a CEO of a major company, his name is Jerry Williams and black folks don't know who he is. He is an absolutely brilliant man and for 10 years he has sat down with me. So if talked about mentors in the sense of a business, that's who I would point to.

These business owners took their future in their own hands and through hard work, persistence, and high motivation were able to succeed. Each in their own way took the bull by the horns, so to speak, and created a future they envisioned. They are living examples of the fact that achievement of your dreams is possible.

Chapter 5

Principle Five

Take ACTION!

"There are risks and costs to a program of action,
but they are far less than the long-range risks
and costs of comfortable inaction."
                                        John Fitzgerald Kennedy

I have learned that success is to be measured not so much by the
position that one has reached in life as by the obstacles which
he has overcome while trying to succeed.
                                        Booker T. Washington

Chapter 5

"There are risks and costs to a program of action,
but they are far less than the long-range risks
and costs of comfortable inaction."

John Fitzgerald Kennedy

I have learned that success is to be measured not so much by the position
that one has reached in life as by the obstacles which he has overcome
while trying to succeed.

Booker T. Washington

Take ACTION!

People who get what they want use Success Strategies

Getting what you want out of life takes more than talent and persistence. You must know when to break with convention and which rules can be broken as part of the journey. There's no need to be ruthless or arrogant in order to achieve this. However, you must be willing to challenge conventional wisdom and to do whatever it takes.

When I first started studying successful people, I realized that their strategies could work for me, too. So set about your journey with these ideas in mind.

Find Your Passion

Many people start out with a passion—a dream—and then spend their lives pursuing it. Others take the time to notice the activities that bring them joy or excite them along the way. There are several steps you can take to find out where your passion lies.

For example:

Pursue information and turn it into knowledge—People sometimes come across their calling by accident. This random opportunity would not have been identified unless they were out in the world exploring, taking risks and accepting challenges.

This kind of serendipity also takes place when you continuously expose yourself to new ideas, new people, new surroundings, new cultures and new sources of inspiration.

Encourage yourself to take risks—Attend networking events and introduce yourself to new people. Ask them questions about their success. They are typically happy to share their knowledge and experience, when asked.

Read books and articles, and take classes to get new ideas, but don't stop there. Become a perpetual learning machine and remember to use your new knowledge so that it becomes transformative learning.

Try activities that are completely new to you. You might find that you have a talent for something you never dreamed possible.

While not every lead you follow will amount to much, sooner or later one of them will point you in a direction that makes the most sense to you. Discover your strengths by asking yourself a series of questions that lead you to find out what you love the most.

For example:

1. Remember three times in your life when you were filled with joy.
2. Remember your three favorite vacations.
3. Identify three accomplishments that made you feel confident in your abilities.
4. Identify three things you are always or often complemented about.
5. Think of three things you'd always loved but think you have outgrown.
6. Identify three things you feel you are really good at.

Check your list to find what these things have in common and use that knowledge to propel you forward.

Also, whenever you find yourself resenting someone else's success or abilities ask yourself this question: "What can I do to motivate myself to this level of success?" Jealousy may veil a good opportunity to learn from other's success. What you can do also, to achieve success, may be there for the viewing.

Fight Procrastination and Inertia

While it is important to have a strategy and goals, don't spend so much time perfecting the plan that you fail to recognize potential opportunities. Rather than getting everything "just so", identify the things that must be done immediately, and then do them. The rest can become long-term goals that you continue to plan for while you work the plan for your short-term goals, and take advantage of low-hanging fruit.

For example, you may not have a college degree or the advanced degree that an opportunity requires, but you may be able to take a certificate program at a local university that costs less and can be completed in a shorter time frame.

If the first step is causing you to procrastinate, then start wherever you can. Start at the end, or in the middle, it doesn't matter. *What really matters is that you start.*

Decide Now to Take Action!

Some years ago, a woman I know wanted to get a college degree, but she thought she was too old. She decided to take classes in the evenings and went to an adult learning program at a local university. She soon found that the evening students were of all different ages and some were as young as her own son. As they worked together in teams she noticed that no-one cared what her age was, and everyone had the same objective: to get a college degree.

She heard about a class that journeyed overseas each year, designed to execute a plan whereby each student would learn in a new and different way than their usual learning style. The students would attend some lectures in the overseas university, but the main objective was to experience a different culture and write about that experience upon their return.

The concept intrigued her. It would impinge on her budget, but as she listened to the students who had taken the trip the year before, and looked through their books and writings, she decided that she was willing to do whatever it took to take this class. So she signed up for the class and soon she was in the Mediterranean and traveling all over Europe to Italy, Spain and Portugal.

During this learning experience, she was so fascinated that she didn't even have time to worry about the cost of the trip. Her roommate was a 22-year old "girl", and she, a woman of 50 years, could have been the roommate's mother. Through this experience, she learned that age didn't matter at all, and that everyone was simply focused on learning, sharing and growing.

Upon her return, she was a changed woman. She had learned so much about herself that was previously unrevealed even to her. This trip was one of the profound experiences of her life, and when the time came to pay for the class, she found that it was well worth the sacrifice.

She was able to achieve the dream of eventually earning her college degree because she decided to *take action* and not put those steps that she *was* able to take. She was able to take the class trip to Europe because she decided to do whatever it took to make that happen. Other steps followed.

By taking action she overcame the inertia that had held her in its grip for 30 years. Moreover, now she has the ability to visit a different country at least once each year for vacation and her own personal satisfaction.

So, what's your excuse? What's holding you back from taking your first step? When you hear that little voice in your head say, "You're too old or you're not smart enough. Or what if I don't fit in? What if I fail? What if they don't like me? What if I'm not good enough?" Take the time to take control of your inner voice and turn this negative self-talk into positive self-talk immediately!

Grandma Moses took up painting when she was 90 years old.

Dennis Rodman was quite unique and a totally different personality from everyone else on the team when he joined the Chicago Bulls basketball franchise. Yet he became a superstar.

Remember that failure is a sign that you at least attempted something. And anyway, what's not to like? You were created in God's image. Ask yourself, "I'm not good enough based on what, and whose criteria?" Tell your inner voice, "Hey, I am great!" There's always a positive answer to shut down any nagging self-doubt or self talk. And you will find that if you practice this rebuttal to any negative self-talk, soon your positive voice becomes an automatic responder to it.

Identify the People Who Can Help You Achieve Your Dreams

While protocol may require that you follow the chain of command or stay within certain channels, this does not mean that the person next in the line of protocol has the ability to help you. The right person is the one who has the ability, knowledge and power to help you advance your goals.

Avoid going through unnecessary channels and focus your efforts on identifying, seeking out and contacting the people who have the experience and clout to help you. Write or fax them a note asking for advice or for the names of people who can help you with your goals.

Be enthusiastic and show your commitment, as this will create a personal commitment from that person. Your enthusiasm not only shows your commitment, but also often brings energy and new excitement to the other person.

Don't Forget the WIIFM Factor

Remember to bring something to the table. WIIFM means "what's in it for me", and is a reminder not to only take from the people who help you, but to give as well. By focusing only on your desires you will be viewed as a taker and not someone who thinks things through to the win-win possibilities of situations.

Before asking for something you want, do some research. Ask questions, yes, but listen carefully to the answers, learning how you can also be helpful to your benefactor. Following up with a thank you note to those who help you also shows your good manners, and etiquette counts.

Set Your Own Limits to No Limits

Remember, the only thing that can hold you back are your own self-limiting beliefs. Don't let what happened to Rod Serling, writer of the television series "The Twilight Zone", happen to you. I wrote these notes on self-doubt while watching Mr. Serling's biography on A&E:

1. Rod Serling sold his "Twilight Zone" television series for $600,000— without even discussing it with his wife! His own modesty in his abilities and self-limiting beliefs became his own undoing. To date, "The Twilight Zone" has grossed over $500 Million.
2. "Night Gallery" was the next show he wrote and he was again filled with self-doubt about his abilities. This show was also a big success.
3. Despite his great success in entertaining those of us watching his shows, his whole life was filled with self-doubt.
4. Because of his self-doubt he and his family lost a fortune, as he did not realize how talented he was or the true value of his work.

Have faith in yourself and know the value of your work!

And while you're dreaming your dreams and setting your course to self-creation, if someone tells you it can't be done remember this poem by Edgar A. Guest. It's a favorite of mine and I hope it will become a favorite of yours too:

EDGAR A. GUEST (1881-1959)

IT COULDN'T BE DONE

Somebody said that it couldn't be done
But he with a chuckle replied
That "maybe it couldn't," but he would be one
Who wouldn't say so till he tried.
So he buckled right in with the trace of a grin
On his face. If he worried he hid it.
He started to sing as he tackled the thing
That couldn't be done, and he did it!

Somebody scoffed: "Oh, you'll never do that;
At least no one ever has done it;"
But he took off his coat and he took off his hat
And the first thing we knew he'd begun it.
With a lift of his chin and a bit of a grin,
Without any doubting or 'quiddit',
He started to sing as he tackled the thing
That couldn't be done, and he did it.

There are thousands to tell you it cannot be done,
There are thousands to prophesy failure,
There are thousands to point out to you one by one,
The dangers that wait to assail you.
But just buckle in with a bit of a grin,
Just take off your coat and go to it;
Just start in to sing as you tackle the thing
That "cannot be done," and you'll do it.

Action is the Key to Success

You never know where opportunity is going to pop up next so you should always be prepared and open to possibilities. Sometimes the required action comes to you in the shower or while driving the car. It may be helpful to carry a small tape recorder with you at all times so that when the idea occurs you are able to capture it immediately.

Some things to think about during self-creation are:

1. Know what your intentions are. Ask yourself, "Do I know my intentions?"
2. What difference does my choice make?
3. Is that difference important in the overall scheme of things?
4. What is more important, the choosing something or the choice I make?
5. Do I know enough about the available options to choose among them?
6. When I don't know enough about the options, is my actual choice really important?

Remember that not making a choice *is* considered making a choice. Your response to these questions will help you to identify which action to take and in what order.

Achievement of your Goal is possible

Use this goal sheet to keep yourself on track.

The Goal	Visualize the outcome you want. Act as if you already have it
Target date	Set a reasonable date for achievement. Then reduce the procrastination through urgency
Motivation	List all emotional reasons to achieve your goal. Ask yourself, "How will this improve the quality of my life?"
Reward	Ask yourself, "What is most important to me in achieving this goal?"

Consequence	What is the consequence of not achieving this goal? How much emotional baggage will continue if you don't proceed with this goal?
Obstacles	Consider how to overcome anything in your way.
Action steps	Formulate a plan. Then work the plan.
Evaluation date	Set a reasonable date to assess how much progress you are making. Reward yourself when you know you are on track.
Completion date	After each accomplishment, celebrate and reward yourself for a job well done.

Where do you plan to be one year from today?

Some of the themes being mentioned here are steps that need to be followed up. You are responsible for your own learning, respecting your desires and meeting your responsibilities to yourself. Some may need to develop a person-to-person relationship with themselves and move from a position style of lack orientation to a position style of achievement orientation, and to cement the importance of a positive environment for learning and using settings, other than the classroom, to expand learning perspectives.

You may need to give yourself pep talks to communicate your values and expectations convincingly. You should try to operate on a person-to-person basis, not a position to position basis.

How well do you treat people? Rub silver and gold together and they get embedded into each other. The same is true of people, so do all you can to be around positive people who make you feel good about yourself. You become what you're around, so surround yourself with the kind of person you wish to be.

Think of your friends and relatives. Are they taking you up or pulling you down? What are you doing for them? If they are pulling you down, maybe its time to move on and surround yourself with positive people who help you feel good about yourself and help you to empower your self-creation.

Make a list of what you will have achieved towards your goal of self-creation a year from now and set about making that happen.

Some examples of things you may want on your list are:

1. What changes do you want to make to your home?
2. What things do you want for your family?
3. Where do you want to go on vacation?
4. What places do you want to visit again?
5. What qualities do you want to have developed or increased?
6. What do you want the reputation of your business to be?
7. What changes do you want to see in your health?
8. What changes do you want in your self-image?
9. What changes do you want in your appearance?
10. What books do you want to read?
11. What books do you want to write?
12. What five people do you want to meet?
13. What business/networking group do you want to speak to?
14. What will your bank account look like a year from today?
15. How far will you have progressed in your self-creation a year from now?

Remember: Your future is in your own hands!

Take action **now** and then measure how much you have achieved in one year's time.

Chapter 6

Principle Six

Initiative—Plant seeds for Personal Achievement

You can learn anything you need to learn to achieve virtually any goal that you can set for yourself. Those who learn, can.
Brian Tracy

Chapter 6

You can learn anything you need to learn to achieve virtually any goal
that you can set for yourself. Those who learn, can.

Brian Tracy

Initiative—Plant Seeds for Personal Achievement

Inner Voice Power

The power of Inner Voice to effect one's physical well being is profound, as I discovered while on one particular consulting engagement. I was to work with a group from a company that had been recently acquired in a merger, their firm having been acquired by my firm. As the team's knowledge expert on the software suite being implemented at a distant client site, I looked forward to all the new challenges that such a glamorous assignment promises.

The voice said, "Oh boy, now I will have the chance to work on a full implementation of this software product. It has taken years to reach this point in my career and I can't wait to get started!"

The rest of the project team was comprised of people from all over the East Coast and Midwest of the United States, and they had worked together before on many, many other projects. They were already friends, but they were meeting me for the first time. Somewhere along the line, a decision was made that I did not belong, did not fit in, and would not be allowed to become a part of their group.

I used every style of communication I had learned thus far in my career, to no avail. Realizing that there were meetings I had missed due to not being invited, I decided to make sure that wouldn't happen again. So I spent every moment with the entire team. We had breakfast together, lunch together, dinner together. I did not even go to the bathroom for the entire day, one day. I had resolved to ensure that I was with them every moment, and I gladly shared all of my knowledge and experience with them. My expertise was accepted, though never acknowledged, but it did not deter me.

None of this changed their behavior, as I found when, eventually I could wait no longer and went to the restroom. As I hurried back I heard them talking—they had used this small window of opportunity alone to have the meeting without me.

"What did I miss?" I asked.

"Nothing," they replied smiling at each other. And so it went for more than six months.

During this time, I commuted by plane from Chicago to Boston every week. The turn around was so fast I did not even have an opportunity to spend time with my precious family. I arrived home at 11:00 p.m. on Thursday nights and departed all too soon on Sunday afternoons by 3:00 p.m. Sadly, There was not enough time to replenish myself at the wellspring of my life.

One morning, I as I got out of bed in the sterile hotel room in Boston, I realized that my foot was hurting. Against a project deadline, I decided to ignore the pain and headed down to the hotel lobby to join the team. I limped all that day and the next, and the day after that. The little voice said, "Maybe you're just getting old." I ignored it and pressed on.

The project ended soon enough, but the pain in my foot did not. I limped my way through all of the ensuing days and nights wondering if the voice was right. Perhaps I was getting old.

"NO!" a different Inner Voice replied, "I'm too young for that to be an option."

"God, I hope I can still wear my high heels, I love them so. I have been wearing them since I was 12 years old and that's the only way I feel comfortable," this different Inner Voice insisted.

I purchased and wore lower heeled shoes, but to no avail. I limped my way through my days and nights and found myself becoming discouraged by how horribly my feet hurt. But I refused to succumb to it. I was certain that I was much too young for this to be happening.

I resolved to overcome the pain through sheer willpower. I soon remembered that I had read somewhere that stress manifests itself in many different ways. This made me become even more determined to "get over it!"

One day after the project completed, and I was back in the corporate office, I was invited to a conference call meeting. I was so excited; I couldn't wait to get there. "This must be my new assignment," I thought. "Now I will be able to use the new skills I've paid so high a price to obtain." Regrettably, that was not to be. My position at the consulting firm that I so loved was unceremoniously cut, eliminated, gone. "Everyone on this conference call is here because we are cutting back on staff. You will be given 2 weeks of severance and I wish you luck in your future endeavors," the manager said.

By this time, the limping became even more exacerbated. I was still determined not to let any of these events get the best of me. I decided on re-scripting the entire incident and refused to let it get the best of me. I took control of my Inner Voice! I told it in no uncertain terms that I refused to believe that I was "getting old" and that "this too shall pass."

Within a month I accepted a position in another firm, with an increase in pay of course, and gradually—as my belief in myself, and my self-confidence returned—the pain in my foot and the limping went away, never to return.

Now I am truly convinced that *stress* had been the cause of all that pain. I had grit my teeth, and endured much hostility and stress to gain the achievement of learning this new technology, and the skill to go forward with it, "by God, whether they helped me or not." In the end, I had paid a hefty price for ignoring the physical signs, and an inner voice left to its own devices. My body had turned against me and made its own statement about the stress I was under by manifesting the pain in my foot, as if to say, "Enough is enough!"

At this point I had been in the United States for over 30 years and this experience was the strongest instance of prejudice that I had ever encountered. Usually it is not so overt. Usually I am able to rise above it without having a physical manifestation of the stress it causes. This time, though, it was so unusual in its relentless cruelty that I don't believe I will ever forget the experience.

I learned a hard lesson from this experience and that project. **Diplomacy and getting along has its place. But, sometimes it's simply not worth the physical and emotional stress, so you should speak up, or get out.**

Luckily, by taking control of my Inner Voice and convincing myself that I was all right and that it was really just stress and I would overcome it, I survived the encounter. Why? Because I *knew* I could do it!

The Wake Up Call

Have you ever had a wake up call? People have them all the time, but not everyone accepts the message that is being delivered when the wake up call comes.

When mine came, I had just returned home the night before, from my mother's 80th birthday party, held in upstate New York.

Going back to Rochester was something I had promised myself that I would never do. But for this special occasion I acquiesced and took the flight back to upstate New York. The place and the people were a curiosity since I had not seen anyone in my family for over a decade. I was going back for a special birthday party that I didn't dare miss. It was just way too special.

It was only hours, but it seemed that days went by before the moment arrived, and when the birthday-lady saw me after more than a decade apart, and realized I had flown in just for this occasion, she burst into tears and put her arms around me, her daughter, and held me in a tight hug. The moment, the moment, the moment . . . it seemed to go on forever. We both shed tears of love and joy at seeing each other after such a long time, an expanse of years with little or no contact.

I felt as much out of place as I had the day I left Rochester, twenty-eight years earlier, and realized that I still did not fit in with this family. Still, I was happy to see her; I had forgotten how beautiful she was.

The following day, I hopped a plane and returned to my "Type A" life. I had been away from my clients for only a few days, but work was always on my mind. I had brought my laptop computer with me even on this trip, and continued to work in the hotel room in the days and hours before my mother's 80th birthday party.

Home again, on that fateful Monday morning, I awoke at 5:00 a.m. as usual and rushed to the shower to start my day. If I were to make the 6:00 a.m. train on time, I would have to hustle.

As the warm water cascaded over me, I felt a little light headed, but paid little attention to it. I had more important things to think about. I remember gripping the showerhead at one point, just to keep my balance, as the light-headedness became stronger.

The next sound I heard was my husband Bill's voice saying, "Are you alright?" His face bore an unfamiliar concerned expression, and he had a hand under each of my arms as he lifted me gently from the floor of the bathtub.

"Did I faint?" I asked, coming around.

"I heard you moaning, and then I heard a big crash! Found you here on the floor of the bath tub," he replied.

"I feel a little dizzy, but I think I'm OK. Just let me sit here for a minute and I'll be fine," I replied, feeling awkward as hell.

It tool me a while to assimilate what had happened. In fact, I had lost consciousness for a minute or two and was just coming around again. Bill rightly forced me to go to the emergency room at a local hospital. If it had been left to me, I would have rested awhile then went to work anyway.

"The client is waiting; this is a critical point in the project. I took Friday off to go to my mother's 80th birthday, so I have a lot of catching up to do," I said to him. Ignoring my protests, Bill drove me to Northwestern Memorial Hospital.

The Hospital

At the emergency room, Bill and I calmly waited until my name was called and then we gave the requisite insurance information. The emergency room receptionist took the information and seemed in no particular hurry to move to the next step: having an actual doctor examined me.

But soon enough, I found myself on a bed, in a curtained off room in the emergency room. As I had always been fearful of hospitals, I was wary of the hospital environment and the illness all around me.

Then, a steady stream of doctors began to come into the room. They took my blood; it was very painful. These days they use plastic disposable needles and somehow, the half asleep nurse kept missing the vein. Before long, my arm was black and blue, but eventually the nurse was able to get some blood for the lab and then insert a saline IV needle with a regulator into my arm.

The steady stream of an emergency room's entourage followed, taking my temperature, checking my heart, my blood pressure, and even performing a cat scan. Some of the tests were so embarrassing I started to cry and was grateful for my husband's ever comforting voice in my ear, and gentle, caring arms around me.

"We're going to keep you overnight and monitor your heart!" the E.R. doctor said.

"I don't have time for this! I have a lot of work to do!" my inner voice argued, and before I knew it, those very words flowed from my lips, unrestrained by reason.

Ignoring my protests, they wheeled my bed upstairs, put me in a room, and admitted me to the hospital. In short order, a whole new parade of nurses began their whole new round of tests. The nurses informed me that, "We will be taking your blood pressure once each hour and we will need to take some more blood." They were definitely taking some more blood, if only to show me who was in charge.

My husband notified my client, and his own employer, that I was admitted to the hospital. Neither of us would be going into work that day.

The doctors and nurses hooked me up to an interminable tangle of wires, and connected them to a computer so that they could monitor my heart for a full 24 hours. They stuck another saline needle in my arm, conveniently mounted on a wheeled stalk, and told me if I needed to move around I should wheel the bottle along with me.

"God I wish I had my computer with me. I've got so much work to do right now, it's making me nuts to just lie here," I said.

Despite the cleverest entreaty that I could conjure, my husband, Bill, refused to get my laptop for me and bring it to the hospital. Dammit, I could have got some work done!

Neither of us had any idea what had happened to me that morning; and so far, the doctors had found nothing.

The Next Day

The next morning, the lead doctor said that the computer showed no anomalies in my system, and that I may be allowed to go home.

"I *have* to go home today. It's the first day of the new class I am teaching at the university and there are almost 20 MBA students already registered for it," I worried aloud. "I've got to get out of here today. Class starts at 6:00 P.M," I continued.

Teaching the class was something I really looked forward to. It would be my first time teaching at this university and the opportunity to work with them was pretty exciting. I was really looking forward to it.

"You need to slow down," the doctor said, "and stop working so much and pushing yourself so hard."

The Test Results

The test results indicated that I had low blood pressure early in the morning, starting around 3:00 a.m. or so, and moving so quickly that morning at 5:00 a.m. had caused me to lose consciousness.

"Get up a little slower in the morning," the doctor advised. "Have a glass of orange juice before starting the day and you will probably be OK," he continued.

Time To Go

They sent me home that day, only 24-hours later, and I was in the classroom teaching my students at 6:00 p.m. that evening.

I did not tell anyone about the event. The university still does not know. My students gave me excellent feedback and just like that, I had started another new career.

Conclusion

The consulting firm I had worked so hard for, putting in 14-hour days with a daily commute to another state, eliminated my job. The market was getting tougher and they we cutting jobs with a vengeance. Nothing personal, this was just business. Just like that, I found myself part of a 10% job cut in another company.

I decided to take it easy for a few weeks and then started a new career as a professional speaker. Now I've embarked on yet another career and love being part of a whole new network of new friends and colleagues.

I have slowed down a bit, and am heeding *the wake up call* that was given to me when God tapped me on the shoulder in the shower one morning. That was a catalyst to writing this book, because I found out that some of my contemporaries are actually dying from the stress related to work and school pressures.

To date five people I know have died of heart attacks and stress related issues. They did not have the benefit of a wake up call. Death just came and took them. Or maybe they got their wake up call, but did not heed it.

The counterfeit inner voice says, "It's time to get to work . . . I could be using my laptop now, on my hospital bed, right now!" It's sounding like an Inner Voice at the time you hear it, but you'll know it's counterfeit by the way it externalizes all of its reason when questioned. "So many people are depending on me."

My true Inner Voice reminded me, "Is it worth it to kill yourself for a job? Look what happened, you lost consciousness and may not have survived, and the net result is, they eliminated your job 'just like that', and they are heedless of any sacrifices or contributions you had made to them and the organization that benefits from your effort."

You'll recognize your true Inner Voice as the one that internalizes its reasons for speaking. "I can't wait to work with these people—the whole idea is really exciting!"

I heeded my wake up call, and believe me, I am grateful for my second chance. Now each day is a gift to enjoy with full appreciation and true joy.

My Inner Voice reminds me "If you're going to work 14-hour days you might as well be doing it for yourself. You have a company you started last year and it was just languishing while you worked so hard for others. Why not focus on your own company and use those skills with small businesses, help them solve business problems just as you did for those big consulting companies who keep downsizing and eliminating the positions of wonderful people like you?"

Sometimes our inner voice wields enormous power. Do you heed the power of your Inner Voice?

What's the Point?

What inner voice am I talking about? I'm talking about the same one that just asked that question. As you go through life and situations occur, or you find yourself in certain situations you ask yourself questions and try to determine the answer to life's issues. Quite often you hear a little voice or a loud voice filled with indignation or hurt reacting to the things you have to deal with, talking to you inside your head—and it drives so many of the decisions that you make. Sometimes you might even ask yourself, "Now why did I say that or why did I do that?" Well, this inner voice has been with you since you were a tiny tot.

We are the sum of all of our experiences, and how we react or don't react or, decide to react to things that occur in life is a direct reflection of the imprinting that we allow to exist in our psyche.

Take me for instance; I was raised to believe that I could do anything I put my mind to. That infers that I have a rational mind and am capable of making decisions based on clarity of vision and expectations. Because I was raised this way, it is second nature for me to attempt new things and to take risks.

This skill is one that can be developed and enhanced, and by using the principles in this book, you will be able to develop it. It already exists, in fact. You have the power. All you have to do is decide to use it—and when you do, you'll discover it can be developed much like building a muscle through exercise. The more you use this skill, the better and stronger it becomes.

What makes you think you can?

When recently interviewed on a television show, the host asked me what made me think I could be a programmer, when I'd decided to enter that field.

My response was instantaneous. "If you think you can't, then you can't, and if you think you can then all of the universe aligns itself to help you to succeed."

To believe you can is the secret of all achievement. Our subconscious mind and our Inner Voice is nothing more than a programming device—much like a computer. What you put in is what you get out. If you feed yourself true belief in yourself and your abilities, then you will find that whatever you believe will be manifested. Yes, some have to work harder than others, but anything reasonable to reach for is worth the effort, even if the reaching becomes the joy. And you may even surprise yourself, one day.

I know, I know, you tell yourself all the time that you believe in yourself and then you fail. But did you really believe in yourself or did you count on outside influences to support your belief? What happens when you tell yourself that you can and then a friend or relative laughs out loud at the thing you dream about? Is your belief in yourself strong enough to withstand their opinion? Is your Inner Voice from them?

Where does this feeling of insecurity come from?

Did you have a parent who told you that you are worthless or even worse—never gave you a kind word about your accomplishments?

When I was employed at Accenture, I met an extremely handsome and intelligent young man. As I watched him in his daily encounters with problems, with clients and other employees, I was impressed with how intelligent and wise he was. One day I told him how great he was with the customers and other employees, and I was surprised at his response.

His eyes softened as he said, "I am surprised at your comments. My father who owns several restaurants thinks that I am stupid. He tells me this all the time, and all my life all I have wanted is for him to be proud of me. But no matter what I do, it is never enough and he is never satisfied, and he still tells me to this day that I am not good enough."

I counseled this special young man for awhile but it all came to nothing, because he had internalized what his father said and his inner voice was adamant in its belief that his father is right.

The secret is that until and unless this young man conquers his true Inner Voice, and takes control of it and re-scripts it to the reality of all of his accomplishments and his abilities, regardless of what his father or anyone else says, he will never be able to reach the level of self actualization that makes him move to the next level that he deserves.

You must take control of your inner voice and use its power to help you move to the next level.

Most people only use the tiniest part of their abilities. When I look at most people I realize that what I am seeing is only the tip of the iceberg where their abilities are concerned. Why they do not realize the heights of achievement that are possible for them still escapes me. Or does it?

You see, it is so much easier to follow the crowd. Our friends, our family tell us who we are, or could be, or what is achievable for us. It takes bravery to say, "I'm going to go for it. I believe in myself and think I can do it. No matter what, I am going for what I want—who I want to be."

The odds seem so great and it is so much more difficult to just "go for it" based only on your own belief. But you know what? History is filled with people who did just that. Think of Colonel Sanders or Bill Gates.

Yes, I know what you're thinking. Based on the portrait the media has painted of Bill Gates for us, you would think he does not fit the profile. But, I was there when he was a little guy with his nose pressed up against the window, tapping on the window of IBM, Big Blue, as they were called in those days, saying, "I have an idea, can I play with you guys? I have this operating system called DOS and I think it will do great things for our culture, for computers, for society and for business. Can I be your partner? Can I play with you?"

And they said, "Go away little boy, [he was very young at the time, in his twenties and I think and a college dropout] we don't need you, what do you know, you are just a kid with an idea and we are IBM—Big Blue. We will develop our own operating system we don't need you. Go away!"

But did he give up? I think I can safely say that everyone knows he did not give up. Today he is in big trouble because *he is bigger than IBM and the richest man in the world.* I know it's an extreme example, but you see, I was there when he was a kid with a dream and no one believed in him but him. He took control of his Inner Voice and now he is the richest man in the world!

Could *you* be the next richest man or woman in the world? Do *you* have an idea that you are afraid to share or implement? What's holding you back?

You must take the initiative and plant the seeds for achievement now. Take control of your Inner Voice and re-program yourself for success. You can do it!

An acquaintance of mine, Jana Stanfield, wrote a song that reminds me I can do it, and it helps to quell the counterfeit inner voice. It goes like this . . .

> *"What would I do if I knew that I could not fail?*
> *If I believed would the wind always fill up my sails?*
> *How far could I go what could I achieve trusting the hero in me?*
> *What steps would I take today, if I were brave?*
> What if we're all meant to do what we secretly dream?
> *What would you ask if you knew you could have anything?*
> *Like the mighty oak sleeps in the heart of a seed are there miracles in*
> *you and me?*
> *If I refuse to listen to the voice of fear, would the voice of courage whisper*
> *in my ear?*
> *What steps would I take today, if I were brave?* [2]

The next time you are afraid to take the initiative and to implement an idea, or take a risk, or take a chance, or try something new, you should ask yourself the question, "What would I do if I knew that I could not fail?" Then go for it.

Plant Shade Trees

While you're working on your self-creation, plant shade trees that you won't sit under. What I mean by this is help someone without the expectation of being reciprocated.

In other words, mentor someone who is not at your level. While we deal with our own personal issues we seldom stop to think that no matter what our level is, there is always someone else who looks up to us, thinks we are doing great, and wishing that we would help them to reach our level of attainment.

When you wonder to yourself, "Oh God, what if they don't like me?" Your Inner Voice should reply, "What's not to like? You're awesome and good at what you do; they'll be lucky to have you." So the next time that little voice starts to say something negative, with self-belief programming, you should hear another voice responding with positive words as your true Inner Voice responds, "That's right, what's not to like!"

And so I offer this strategy to you: arm yourself with positive self talk and whenever you hear that little voice say anything negative. Immediately, and I mean immediately, re-script whatever that counterfeit inner voice said, into something positive—your true Inner Voice will pipe up soon enough.

---

[2] "If I were brave" Jana Stanfield *www.JanaStanfield.com*

It's amazing how when you take the initiative and plant seeds of achievement and turn negative self-talk into positive self talk, how good things ensue. And the best thing is, by changing negative self talk into positive self-talk consistently, eventually it becomes automatic, until when negativity or negative self talk rears its ugly head, it's recognizable, is instantly quelled being immediately replaced by positive self talk.

Soon you will find yourself being positive consistently and having greater expectations, healthy self-esteem and believe me, people will notice. You will too, because you will begin to attract good and positive things and people into your life.

Chapter 7

Principle Seven

Now is the time to Achieve Your Dreams

You don't have to take life the way it comes to you. By converting your dreams into goals, and your goals into plans, you can design your life to come to you the way you want it. You can live your life on purpose, instead of by chance.
                                    ~ Whatever it takes—"The Goal"

Chapter 7

You don't have to take life the way it comes to you. By converting your dreams into goals, and your goals into plans, you can design your life to come to you the way you want it. You can live your life on purpose, instead of by chance.

~ Whatever it takes—"The Goal"

Now Is the Time to Achieve Your Dreams

So, you're thinking of changing careers . . .

How many careers would you say you have had to date? One? Two or more? In America, our parent's generation seldom considered changing careers. The career model for their time was to join a company, work their way up through the ranks by virtue of promotions and retire with a great pension. Loyalty to the company was the byword, with an expectation that this quality would be valued by the company. At their retirement party, they might even get a gold watch and be sent on their way to care-free golden years. Changing careers was not even on the radar screen for most professionals back then.

Today, companies see a potential issue if a professional has not changed careers at least once. By careers I mean moving from one field to another, or moving to different industries and functional positions within a field.

Sure, programmers may transition to technical leads and technical leads to project managers or system architects. But they may also transition from computer technician to marketing manager. They may apply their skills to manufacturing industries at one time in their work life and to a law firm in the next. This is a fairly standard practice in the career track of today's professional worker, but these transitions should always be planned if they are to be a successful.

Quite often, however, when considering a career change the totality of the responsibilities of the new position are largely unknown. Happily, there are several methods currently used by corporations that enable employees to "try on" a position before making the career change. For example, you can "shadow" someone who works in the field you wish to move to thus enabling you to see what a typical day or week is really like in that job. Sometimes, you will find on closer inspection that the job is nothing like you thought or the requirements are such that further education or longer work hours are required. This method allows you to see in advance what the job is really like without having to give up your current position. Indeed, this style of checking out a career change first is a good idea if you are not quite sure which position is right for you.

I once undertook an interesting research exercise during my undergrad studies that required each student to thoroughly research their "dream job". If you didn't have to worry about the time, money, or emotional support needed to get there, what would be your "dream job"? What do people who have such jobs really do every day? The most fascinating aspect of this assignment was to hear many of my classmates adopt a newfound appreciation for what was really involved in the doing of their "dream job", and then to proclaim that, "This is no longer something I want to do."

Sometimes additional training is required for the career move and it behooves the person making the change to do a thorough investigation prior to executing the investment of time and money. Your company may be prepared to pay for your training since your improved skills will benefit you both. In order for the company to remain competitive in the marketplace, they realize they need up to date skills. Similarly, benefits like additional training cuts down on attrition, which can be very costly.

Another alternative is to seek out a mentor in an association or professional organization who already works in the field of interest, and spark a conversation to determine the personality characteristics required for the position. For example, a systems developer who is considering moving to call center work may find that interaction with the public in a customer service role is not compatible with their personality. Whereas a continued role in the development area, moving to architect of a software module, for instance, more naturally suits their personality and style of working.

Each individual must find their own motivation and determine whether the desire to change careers is based on sound reasoning. Among other things, people need to verify whether they are in the wrong career or if the motivation to change careers is based solely on monetary compensation or because something is amiss in their personal lives.

Prior to executing a career change I suggest that you put together a list of your career expectations. For instance, if you could have any job you want, what would it be?

Put together a list of things you would like to do that are unmet in your current position. Look around your present company to see what position could provide you with more job satisfaction. Then thoroughly research it to see if the job is what you think it is.

Chapter 8

Principle Eight

Grow yourself and your talents— recognize the gifts of the universe

Sow an Act and you reap a Habit
Sow a Habit and you reap a Character
Sow a Character and you reap a Destiny
Open yourself to the abundance of the Universe

Chapter 8

Sow an Act and you reap a Habit
Sow a Habit and you reap a Character
Sow a Character and you reap a Destiny
Open yourself to the abundance of the Universe

Grow Yourself and Your Talents— Recognize the Gifts of the Universe

Identify your idea of what success is for you, and who you wish to become. What is important to you?

As you begin the journey of self-creation, step back and identify what is important to you. It may be that family is your top priority; or perhaps raising well-adjusted healthy children who will contribute meaningfully to society is where your interests lie. It might even be that at the current moment your career, a change of career, finally getting that degree or achievement of a stress free life is your reason for self-creation.

Regardless of the impetus that brought you here and made you consider self-creation, there are specific steps you can take that will ensure you are successful in the process.

Use the following 15 points to do a self—evaluation for self creation:

1. *Create constancy of purpose for personal improvement:* Redefine yourself, then determine what needs to be done to get from who you are to who you want to be. Then act as if you are that person.
2. *Adopt a new philosophy:* Don't accept anything less than the best that life has to offer

3. *Cease dependence on Mass Approval:* Don't spend time and money on items for others approval. Determine what is best for *you* and spend time and energy on improving yourself. Listen to your Inner Voice!

4. *End the practice of making decisions based on short term results or others evaluation of your choices:* instead of asking for approval from the outside, ask yourself what is right for me now in order to move from where I am to where I want to be.

5. *Improve yourself constantly and forever with a systemized process of productive use of your time and your abilities:* Manage your time and look at time wasters such as watching TV. Improve the quality of time spent with yourself.

6. *Institute training:* Identify where training is needed to get you to where you want to be and who you want to become. Get training formally and the right way rather than by word of mouth. Seek out others who have successfully transitioned and collaborate with them or ask them to be your mentor as you move through your transition.

7. *Institute Leadership:* Regardless of where you are in your process of self-creation, there are always others who look at you and think how great you are doing. Share your skills and abilities with others and help to pull them up to where they want to be. If you are a great cook share your recipe, teach someone to speak a different language, help younger students to learn how to learn. It doesn't matter what it is, the important thing is to share your knowledge and expertise. This is how you master your leadership skills.

8. *Drive out fear:* It is necessary for self-creation to believe that you can do it and to believe in yourself.

If you think you can't, then you won't be able to achieve your desires no matter how hard you try. If you think you can and work at achievement, then you can. Your subconscious mind believes whatever you tell it, and if you think you can, then at a subconscious level you will always be working on it—whether you realize it or not. Just keep at it and one day you will have mastered whatever it is and you will realize that it has become natural for you.

Many very successful people are afraid, but the trick that they have mastered is to feel the fear and do it anyway. Children are a great example of this. They feel the fear and try new things anyway, usually succeeding.

Many well known performers like Johnny Carson, Barbara Streisand, and other performers that people admire, perform onstage even though they are petrified every time. Lee Iacocca is well known in public speaking circles for his technique whenever he feels "butterflies in his stomach" . . . "The trick is to get them to fly in formation."

9. *Break down barriers between where you are and where you want to be:* Too often people compete with each other rather than with themselves. The great athletes become great because they realize that what they have to beat is their own last accomplishment.

10. *Eliminate slogans, exhortations and targets set by others for your achievement:* Create your own slogan and put it up. Create your own mission and vision statement and work on achieving those.

    My mission is to awaken dreams and inspire self—creation. I am working towards its fulfillment. Though told by many that it is a lofty dream, I thank them and press on because it is *my* dream and my mission.

11. *Realize that your dream is important:* Never let weeds grow over your dreams, cultivate them and water them with positive thoughts and ideas every day.

12. *Remove barriers to pride in your achievement of your dreams:* You want to do a good job for your family, your children, your job and yourself. Eliminate misguided comments from anyone who does not encourage you toward the fulfillment of your dreams.

13. *Institute a vigorous program of education and retraining:* Regardless of where you are in life, no one knows everything. Seek out opportunities to get more education in a new method of doing things, including teamwork and new techniques. Every day when we wake up, we find there is some new technology that has changed our world. Educate yourself to stay on top of things. It could be as simple as a new technology that runs the car but it touches you and you life anyway. Every time you master a new skill, every time you master a new task, you are enabling self-creation and becoming a better you.

14. *Focus on solutions:* One of my first mentors told me, "Don't bring me problems, I have enough problems of my own. Bring me solutions!" The best way to do this is to research the problem, determine the solution and put the whole thing together as though you are presenting a proposal to a client. This allows the mind to execute the full lifecycle of the means to the solutions and on results. When you approach the gap between where you are and where you want to be in this manner, you will find success in moving to the next level is expedited.

15. *Take action to accomplish the transformation:* Form a specific plan of action to carry out the mission of moving from where you are to where you want to be.

A powerful story of self-creation

In 1999, while still in the Air Force and based in Okinawa, my son Charles sent a story to me. It was a great motivator for me, and I hope you find it motivating too. Its moral is that two people can make such a great difference, even in the face of complacency and adversity.

It must be noted here, that there is no way to confirm the authenticity of this story, and this author has the highest respect for Ivy League universities.

You Can't Judge a Book by its Cover

A lady in a faded gingham dress and her husband, him dressed in a homespun, threadbare suit, stepped off the train in Boston and walked timidly without an appointment into an Ivy League university President's outer office.

His secretary could tell in a heartbeat that such backwoods, country hicks had no business at a university campus and probably didn't even deserve to be on the prestigious Boston campus.

She frowned as the man said softly, "We want to see the President."

"He'll be busy all day," the secretary snapped.

"We'll wait," the lady replied.

For hours, the secretary ignored them, hoping that the couple would finally become frustrated and go away. They didn't, and the secretary reluctantly decided to disturb the President, even thought this was a chore she abhorred.

"Maybe if they just see you for a few minutes, they'll leave," she suggested.

He sighed in exasperation and nodded. Someone of his importance obviously didn't have the time to waste with them, but he detested gingham dresses and homespun suits, the thought of which, cluttering up his outer office, bordered on the grotesque.

The President, stern-faced with dignity, strutted toward the couple.

The lady told him, "We had a son who attended the university for one year. He loved it. He was happy here. But about a year ago, he was accidentally killed. Now my husband and I would like to erect a memorial to him somewhere on campus."

The President wasn't touched by her story. Instead he was shocked.

"Madam," he said gruffly, "we can't put up a statue for every person who attended our university and died. If we did, this place would look like a cemetery."

"Oh, no," the lady explained quickly. "We don't want to erect a statue. We thought we would like to give a building to the university."

The President rolled his eyes. He glanced at the gingham dress and homespun suit, and then he exclaimed, "A building! Do you have any earthly idea how much a building costs? We have over seven and a half million dollars in the physical plant at this university."

For a moment the lady was silent. The President was pleased. He could get rid of them now.

The lady turned to her husband and said quietly, "Is that all it costs to start a university? Why don't we start our own?" Her husband nodded.

The President's face wilted in confusion and bewilderment.

And Mr. and Mrs. Leland Stanford walked away, traveling to Palo Alto, California, where they established the university that bears their name—a memorial to a son that Harvard no longer cared about.

You can easily judge the character of others by how they treat those who can do nothing for them or to them. [3]

From a gingham dress and a homespun threadbare suit—and a dream for a lost son—this couple bridged the gap between where they were and the manifestation of their dream, and today Stanford University is well known as one of the best universities in the country.

Recognize the gifts of the universe

Never let weeds grow around your dreams. Identify the gap, build a bridge to your dream and sail off into the possibility and the future that you want, create it yourself.

When you make the commitment to fulfillment of your dreams, don't be surprised as the universe shares its abundance with you. It seldom fails.

There is an abundance of energy in the universe that is virtually inexhaustible. What you throw to it is what you receive from it. What you dream is possible becomes what your future is filled with. The power of your own mind is unfathomable.

Once you have made your decision, give yourself a PEP talk every day. That means **P**ossibilities, **E**xpectations, and **P**ersistence. Use the form below to write down your daily PEP talk now.

Possibilities: The Possibility I am inventing for myself is:

_____

_____

_____

_____

_____

My Expectation is:

_____

_____

_____

_____

_____

---

[3]   Malcolm Forbes [from a letter from my son Charles 7/6/99]

My Persistence will consist of:

_____

_____

_____

_____

_____

_____

I invite your to *consider the possibilities* and *see what happens.*

Where you are and where you want to be is a reflection. The you that everyone sees is a reflection of your thoughts and your own self talk. To inspire self-creation you must first harness the power of your true Inner Voice and change negative self-talk into positive self-talk the moment you hear it. The minute your Inner Voice hears even the hint of negative self-talk, immediately replace it with your daily PEP talk.

Live your life on purpose instead of by chance. Make a contract now with *yourself* about the new purpose of your life and watch how the universe works with you towards its achievement.

Chapter 9

Principle Nine

Motivation and Persistence will Make Your Dreams a Reality

You contain within yourself a unique combination of talents and abilities which, properly identified and applied, will enable you to achieve virtually any goal you can set for yourself.
What parts of your work do you enjoy the most and are you the best at? This is your best indicator of your true talents.

Brian Tracy

Chapter 9

You contain within yourself a unique combination of talents and abilities which, properly identified and applied, will enable you to achieve virtually any goal you can set for yourself.
What parts of your work do you enjoy the most and are you the best at? This is your best indicator of your true talents.

Brian Tracy

Motivation and Persistence Will Make Your Dreams a Reality

But be careful of the fakes selling snake oil

A major requirement for successful self-creation is the ability to remain motivated in the face of obstacles, naysayers and adversity. Sometimes menace comes without warning, to leave you reeling in its wake as it charges like a speedboat through the calm waters of your belief in yourself.

Maggie was one of those buoyant women who could always be counted on to rise to the occasion whenever there was need of a helping hand for a constructive aim. Maggie attended many networking events, involving herself tenaciously, and especially in those groups dedicated to women helping women.

One evening, Maggie was approached by Heather who invited her to join a group of female entrepreneurs who meet monthly to discuss business and help each other to achieve their dreams of running successful companies. Maggie was delighted at the prospect of meeting and sharing with other women who were also entrepreneurs and could scarcely wait until the first meeting.

This group, the Women's Business Development Center, is intended to help women entrepreneurs and to mentor them to be successful. It is funded by the state to ensure that women have the opportunity for self-creation if they have a business idea.

Finally, the meeting day arrived, and Maggie drove into the city eager to learn and grow and share. It was tricky and difficult to locate a parking space in the subterranean world of the now cavernous city, but since she had arrived early she had time to wait for a spot. Finally parking in the dankest of corners, she noted that she may have to lay down a trail of bread crumbs to find this particular location again, but decided to put that thought behind her as she climbed to the street and welcome sunlight. She soon realized that the meeting location was farther than she thought, but she didn't care much, choosing instead to stride confidently and blissfully up the busy street. She navigated between the lunchtime crowds as best she could, until she located the building, which she noticed had a food court in its own belly. She purchased a lunch for herself, and bringing it upstairs, she located the meeting room and was pleased to see the other women she knew were already there.

It was a good turnout for any group, and as each woman took her turn to introduce herself and describe her business, Maggie knew that she had found just what she needed. Here was a place where a new entrepreneur could learn and grow from those who had already attained a certain level of success.

One woman had 50 employees and she described how she attracted clients in the early days and the strategies she used to become successful. Another woman brought a copy of her niche software product and explained how the concept and vision worked. A third woman spoke of how she did not use venture capital companies because they sometimes treat her like a child and she preferred to express her own vision.

Maggie was intrigued and excited, and being a quick learner left the meeting, her head bursting with ideas, joy in her heart and a skip in her step. She wondered if people could notice the smile on her face and found she couldn't stop grinning all day.

After attending about five such meetings, the e-mail that next arrived in her inbox must be a change in who would be hosting the next meeting, she thought. She thought wrong . . .

Maggie was invited to *not* return to the sixth meeting, the e-mail informed her. Maggie wondered the better part of a day before getting in touch with the sender of the e-mail. All sorts of thoughts were going through her mind, and she needed to find out if there was some fault in her that she might correct.

"Why am I no longer welcome?" she asked?

"Because you will never hire other employees and so you don't fit the profile of the women we want in our group." The e-mail's author replied.

"Well, I may not have employees right now, but I do plan on growing the company to have employees later on," Maggie explained.

"I'm not going to argue with you," the voice on the phone replied. "And anyway I guess the members will be weeded out by attrition anyway."

"Does this mean that Patricia will not be attending anymore either? I mean, she does not have employees either," Maggie countered.

"Pat is welcome to continue attending, she is on the Mayor's Technology Committee, so she has connections that she can use to help us," the voice replied.

"OK, I understand completely," Maggie groaned. Then she hung up.

As she considered the situation, Maggie's head was filled with the sounds of her inner voice going—over the events of the last few hours—and she felt herself beginning to feel sad.

"Too bad," she thought. "Too bad that they threw the baby out with the bathwater. I'll show them how wrong they are, and I won't allow them to discourage me, or step on my dreams."

"Why don't you give yourself a PEP talk," her Inner Voice told her. "You're always saying that people should give themselves a PEP talk and harness the power of their inner voice. Why don't you use it yourself to overcome this disappointment?"

A big smile spread across her face, as Maggie decided to use the opportunity to reaffirm her commitment to herself and her company instead. As she considered the Possibilities, Expectations and the Persistence that she would use as a strategy for success, she knew that it might be much more dangerous to belong to such a group, their priorities being what they are.

Soon the bright sunshine of a great knowledge enveloped Maggie's whole being as she felt her step get a little lighter, her stride become a little stronger, and she heard her Inner Voice start to sing a joyful song. Maggie had learned that even sometimes the people who purport themselves most to be your biggest constituent, are themselves, listening to a counterfeit inner voice.

Be careful of the fakes.

Have you failed at anything lately?

Have you failed at anything lately? If not, then perhaps you are not taking risks or stretching yourself enough. In order to fail, you must have tried to do something new. That usually results in either a new success or an opportunity to learn from failure.

"Our strength," Ralph Waldo Emerson said, "grows out of our weakness. Not until we are pricked and stung and sorely shot at, awakens the indignation which arms itself with secret forces. A great man is always willing to be little. Whilst he sits on the cushion of advantages he goes to sleep. When he is pushed, tormented, defeated, he has a chance to learn something; he has been put on his wits, on his manhood; he has gained facts; learned his ignorance; been cured of the insanity of conceit; he has got moderation and real skill."

Think of the people you have known personally who failed at one thing, only to press on and continue to achieve great success at something else. Defeat is not final, it is not a destination. It is just a line in the road that must be crossed while on the journey.

To encourage you in your journey I include here some of the most famous winners who failed or suffered defeat and didn't give up.

1. Walt Disney received 302 rejections for financing loans for Disney World
2. The manager of the Grand Ole Opry with the statement, "Son you ain't going anywhere," and fired Elvis!
3. Albert Einstein was originally rejected from his first choice round university on the grounds that he showed no promise.
4. H. R. Macy failed 7 times before his store Macy's of New York succeeded.
5. Colonel Sanders, the founder of Kentucky Fried Chicken, spent more than 2 years traveling around in an old car trying to sell his chicken recipe before he got any takers. He was rejected 1,009 times before he found a buyer. But today his restaurants are in virtually every town in America, and now global.
6. The legendary Marshall Field is said to have had his store burn completely to the ground at least twice. When the other storeowners decided to move to a different location, he said, "I will rebuild my store on this same spot, bigger and better than ever!" And he did! Today thousands are bussed in during the Thanksgiving and Christmas holidays to gaze in wonder at the decorations in his store window. This store is still one of the most often visited on State Street, Chicago, Illinois. U.S.A
7. Jack Canfield received over 170 rejections for his book, "Chicken Soup for The Soul" and yet today it has sold over 70 million copies. The book has also spawned multiple chicken soup series books, a road show, and a television show and continues to grow and appeal to people all over the world.

Persistence is the key to success

These people succeeded because they persisted. They refused to give up and so should you refuse to give up as well. If they persisted, and succeeded, so can you.

Persistence measures the lengths to which you will go to succeed. It reflects your commitment and refines your character and ultimately it will lead to your success.

President Coolidge once stated: "Nothing in the world will take the place of perseverance. Talent will not, nothing is more common than unsuccessful men with talent. Genius will not, unrewarded genius is almost a proverb. Education, will not, the world is full of educated derelicts. Persistence and determination alone are omnipotent.

With the unlimited power of persistence on your side *You Can Do It*!

Starting today think of what you would do if you knew that you could not fail. Write it down and get to work. At the end of the day, take stock in your accomplishments.

I guarantee you will have made progress. And this progress will become an incredible self-esteem builder that underscores the fact that *You Can Do it!*.

Chapter 10

Principle Ten

Enjoy the New You

I was restless. I was doing okay, but I was restless. One day it dawned on me that I had been looking at life through the wrong end of the telescope. It was up to me to turn it around—to make it bigger, better, more satisfying.

Arnold Schwarzenegger

Chapter 10

I was restless. I was doing okay, but I was restless. One day it dawned on me that I had been looking a life through the wrong end of the telescope. It was up to me to turn it around—to make it bigger, better, more satisfying.

Arnold Schwarzenegger

Enjoy the New You

Your success is in your own hands!

Practice leadership skills

The new you should make a difference. This is how to be truly successful in your new career and in your personal life. Now that you are here, congratulate yourself and do a self-assessment of your leadership skills.

Consider what you bring to the table—Indulge a bit and consider what you have:

> ➤ Talent? Everyone is really, really good at something.
> ➤ Enthusiasm? Even in the face of adversity, enthusiasm makes sense.
> ➤ A measurable skill set that has value in the marketplace? Got it or get it, this one should be easy . . . are you measuring it?
> ➤ Initiative? Getting off the dime is the key.
> ➤ Motivation? Figure your reasons for doing things using your true Inner Voice
> ➤ Are you an idea generator? I bet you are!
> ➤ Are you a jiggler? A jiggler joins in and just shakes things up, or bangs things that stopped working. They don't necessarily make waves. They ask questions and bring their experiences to the table so that oftentimes an organization is shaken out of complacency by fresh new, or even

old ideas. The "all of a sudden, things started working again all by themselves" was most likely set off by a "jiggler."

I like to think of leadership as A=PIE. That means:

Leadership = Adaptability, Persuasiveness, Initiative and Empathy.

To be successful, *focus on the things that matter most.*

Ask yourself:

1. What is my mission?

   _____

   _____

   _____

   _____

   _____

   _____

2. What is right for *now*?

   _____

   _____

   _____

   _____

   _____

   _____

3. Review your goals.

   _____

   _____

   _____

   _____

   _____

   _____

4. Review your roles.

   _____

   _____

   _____

   _____

   _____

   _____

Use the 4 leadership skills:

1. Initiative
2. Empathy
3. Adaptability
4. Persuasiveness

If you integrate these four behaviors into your communication with others you will find others are more likely to be supportive.

Use facilitative skills

Help your colleagues and team members to discover their own answers—use these types of questions:

1. What are your thoughts?
2. What was your thought process, so I can understand?
3. How can we accelerate your response time?

These are the secrets of being a facilitator. What is the difference between speaking and facilitating? In speaking the mouth is viewed as the primary instrument. In facilitation the EARS and the MIND are viewed as the primary instruments.

Use the R2A2 formula and opportunity awareness to bring new ideas to the table.

R2A2 means "Recognize and Relate, Assimilate and Apply".

Recognize and Relate

Learn to *recognize* common threads, trends or opportunities to use what appears to be a seemingly innocuous item and *relate* it to your business, company, product or career.

Carry a notebook or use a palmtop organizer, but write down your ideas without delay. Ideas are fragile and can die from lack of attention. By writing down new ideas immediately, you preserve the seeds that you can nurture and grow later on.

Assimilate and Apply

Contemplate and consider the feasibility of the idea, don't do anything yet, and then actuate.

Assimilate the new idea—think about it and absorb it.

Finally, apply and follow through to the idea's birth and fruition. Then apply the new behavior or the new principles to your product, career or personal life.

You may even find yourself creating a new product other than the new you that you have self-created.

If you do find that you have a new idea you wish to present, put it together as a proposal and present it as through to a client. Have it well laid out so that when you converse others will see that you have already done your homework and what you propose is largely ready to go. Believe me, they are more likely to listen to your idea and support your proposal if you're organized and prepared.

Points to remember:

Leadership deals with determining a direction.

Management deals with speed, coordination, logistics and going in a direction.

Leadership is visionary, strategic, effective and adaptable.

By using the R2A2 formula and the leadership=APIE strategy, you can add value to others ideas as well as your own.

Chapter 11

Daily reading of the following passages will help you in your plan for Self Creation

The Law of Abundance

We live in an abundant universe where there is an ample supply of money for all those who really want it.

To achieve financial independence, make a decision today to accumulate wealth and then do what others have done before you to accomplish the same goal

Brian Tracy

Chapter 11

The Law of Abundance

We live in an abundant universe where there is an ample supply of money for all those who really want it.

To achieve financial independence, make a decision today to accumulate wealth and then do what others have done before you to accomplish the same goal

Brian Tracy

Daily reading of the "1459 Plan" can help support your plan for Self Creation

The 1459 Plan

For a minimum of 14 minutes and 59 seconds daily, read, memorize and internalize the following five items selected and included here for your inspiration:

- ➤ W. Clement Stone's "17 Principles of Success"
- ➤ PMA—Positive Mental Attitude
- ➤ James J Mape's "CVS to BVS"
- ➤ The R2A2 Principle
- ➤ Vision and Achievement

W. CLEMENT STONE'S
17 PRINCIPLES OF SUCCESS

1. Positive Mental Attitude
2. Definiteness of Purpose
3. Going the Extra Mile
4. Accurate Thinking
5. Self-Discipline
6. The Master—Mind Alliance
7. Applied Faith
8. A Pleasing Personality
9. Personal Initiative
10. Enthusiasm
11. Controlled Attention
12. Teamwork
13. Learning From Defeat
14. Creative Vision
15. Budgeting Time and Money
16. Maintaining Sound Physical and Mental Health
17. Cosmic Habit Force [4]

Examine these 17 principles for a minimum of five (5) minutes daily. Go over them until they are internalized and they become a habit, and you will find yourself living a life of principles that bring you success. Remember that success can be measured in many ways other than monetarily; it is also found in other aspects of the quality of our lives.

Have A Positive Mental Attitude

Many of the things in life that happen to us are beyond our control. How we allow them to affect us, however, is one thing that *is* certainly within our control. How we choose to react to these events is the sole determinant of the true outcome. If we live life using the principle of a Positive Mental Attitude, we can turn adversity into opportunity.

According to W. Clement Stone, we have within us, a magic talisman with PMA (Positive Mental Attitude) emblazoned on one side and NMA (Negative Mental Attitude) on the other. The state of our minds when an adversity occurs directly impacts which side of the talisman will be visible. If it is NMA then we will attract more negativity and repel the possible positive outcomes. If it is PMA then we will attract more positive events and outcomes.

---

[4] Believe and Achieve, Cypert, Samuel A

On a recent visit to Spain, I was shocked to see that some gypsies lived in cave-like holes in the mountains. We were told to be careful of them, but I found them fascinating. I took a picture of a gypsy who stopped by our table at an outdoor cafe and played the most incredible flamenco music on his guitar. His posture radiated his obvious PMA. This was just more proof to me that it is not your circumstances in life, but how you choose to live the life you have that counts.

So I say to you, it is time that you meet the most important living person. The day you determine a positive mental attitude for yourself is the day that you will meet the most important living person! Who is that? Well, the most important living person is *you*, as far as *you and your life* are concerned. Take a look at yourself. Isn't it true that you carry with you an invisible power that only you can use effectively for your own well-being? What exactly is this power, this force? The power is your subconscious mind and the control you have over your inner voice.[5]

What's that you say? How can you have a positive mental attitude when there are so many negative things happening in our society today? No one ever promised us the world would be perfect. In fact it has never been perfect, but that fact has never stopped individuals from creating wealth and success for themselves.

In today's global economy there are myriad ways to be successful. It is up to *you* to determine what success means to you. Is it a title in your profession? Is it raising healthy, well-adjusted children who will contribute positive things to society? Is it monetary, or is it reaching self-actualization? Only you can decide. These are things to keep in mind on your journey to self-creation. By determining your own definition of success, you will be able to determine when you have achieved it, and if your daily actions are supportive of your desired destination.

What I offer you here is the roadmap to PMA that W. Cement Stone shared with the world decades ago. I found that using it to helps me to learn and grow, and I now share it with you. I offer you Mr. Stone's "Thoughts to Steer By" to incorporate into your daily inspiration as part of the 1459 PLAN.

THOUGHTS TO STEER BY

Meet the most important living person! That person is *you*. Your success, health, happiness, wealth depend on how you use your invisible talisman. How will you use it? The choice is yours.

Your mind is your invisible talisman. The letters PMA (Positive Mental Attitude) are emblazoned on one side and NMA (Negative Mental Attitude) on the other. These are powerful forces. PMA *is the right mental attitude for each specific occasion.* It has the power to attract the good and the beautiful. NMA repels them. It is a negative mental attitude that robs you of all that makes life worth living.

---

[5] Success through a Positive Mental Attitude; Hill, Napoleon and Stone, W. Clement

Self question: How can I develop the right mental attitude? Be specific.

Don't blame God for your lack of success. Like countless others you can develop a burning desire to succeed. How? *Keep your mind on the things you want and off the things you don't want.* How?

Read inspirational books for a purpose. Ask for divine guidance. *Search for the light.*

Self question: Do you believe it's proper to ask for divine guidance?

Every adversity has the seed of an equivalent or greater benefit for those who have PMA. Sometimes the things that seem to be adversities turn out to be *opportunities in disguise.*

Self question: Will you engage in thinking time to determine how you can turn adversities into seeds of equivalent or greater benefit?

Accept the priceless gift—*the joy of work.* Apply the greatest value in life: *love people and serve them.* You will attract big and generous portions of success. You can if you develop PMA.

Self question: Will you search to find out how you can develop PMA as you read the 1459 PLAN?

Never underestimate the repellant power of a negative mental attitude. It can prevent life's lucky breaks from benefiting you.

Self question: PMA attracts good luck. How can I develop the habit of PMA?

You can profit by disappointment—if it is turned into inspirational dissatisfaction, with PMA. Develop *inspirational dissatisfaction.* Rearrange your attitudes and convert a failure of one day into success on another. How do you think you can develop inspirational dissatisfaction?

Bring into reality the possibility of the improbable by acquiring PMA. Say to yourself as Henry Ford said to his engineers, *"keep working!"*

Self question: Have you the courage to aim high and strive daily to keep your goal before you?

Don't make your mental attitude make you a "has been." When you become successful and a depression or any other unfavorable circumstance arises which causes you a loss or defeat, act on the self-motivator: *Success is achieved by those who try, and maintained by those who keep trying with PMA.* This is the way to avoid being crushed. [6]

UNIVERSAL PRINCIPLES IN SELF-MOTIVATOR FORM

1. Every adversity has within it the seeds of an equivalent or greater benefit
2. Greatness comes to those who develop a burning desire to achieve high goals.
3. Success is achieved and maintained by those who try and keep on trying with PMA

[6] Success Through A Positive Mental Attitude; Stone, W. Clement; Hill, Napoleon

4. To become an expert achiever in any human activity, it takes practice . . . practice . . . practice . . .
5. Man's greatest power lies in the power of prayer [7]

Current View of the Situation To Better View of the Situation

I include here the CVS to BVS motivator because with its discovery I found freedom. One of the methods I use to help me maintain equilibrium, a healthy perspective, and to grow, is to seek out and read inspirational books and tapes.

My method, though not scientific, is to go to the bookstore and simply wander along the isle of inspirational books and tapes. If I find something that piques my interest, I pick it up and read the outline of what the author presents for inspiration.

It was on one such trip that I located the treasure of a book called "Quantum Leap Thinking", by James J. Mapes. I had never heard of Mr. Mapes before but found the description of what was contained in the tape to be immediately uplifting. I quickly snapped up the only audio copy and took my treasure home.

On Monday morning, as is my usual routine, I loaded the tape in my car stereo and prepared to start my day with an inspirational message that would set the tone for my mindset and take my mind off the traffic and long ride to the office.

I cannot express enough, the joy listening to this series of tapes brought to me. I especially related to the author's statement that I would listen to the tapes and walk away with whatever I found of interest while the rest would not have the same impact.

At first, I thought, oh no not me, this is all too valuable. However, as time past and I returned to re-listen to the tape, I realized that I had indeed missed many ideas that I now found of interest and decided that I would write down these new nuggets of value to ensure that I would not forget.

One morning, after an incident I perceived as a failure, I put in Mapes' audio tape to boost my mood and lift my spirits and found the golden nugget I offer as part of the 1459 plan. He calls it changing CVS to BVS and it goes like this:

Let's call your point of view your current view of the situation, or your CVS. The current view of the situation is simply how, at this very moment, you define specific goals or expectation, and your CVS is controlled totally by your perceptions.

You create your CVS and because you create it, you can create something different, something better. You can take your CVS and alter it into a better

---

one. You have the choice to create a far better view of the situation (BVS) and if you do you, will find that your mood will change.[8]

I was exhilarated! I tried it, and the response in my mood was instantaneous. I added it to my daily affirmations and found that it never fails me, and that's why it is included as part of the 1459 plan.

Say the words, "change my current view of the situation to a better view of the situation" a hundred times a day. Or as Mapes put it, "Use the easier form CVS to BVS", then when those moments of self-doubt arise you can convert them from something negative to a better view of the situation—to something positive that can be used for inspiration.

How I Use the R2A2 Formula

I have always had a burning desire to own my own company. But what type of company would it be, and how do I articulate to my clients the values and benefits the company offers?

After being downsized many times, I found myself filled with a profound feeling of sadness each time the media announced that more jobs were being cut. I realized that there was a void of leadership for those downsized individuals and nothing was ever offered to them in the way of pulling their life and careers back together.

These downsized individuals were on their own. It was then that I decided that my company would bring hope to them and supply them with the tools to motivate and inspire them to not only find new positions, but to arm them with the skills to quickly rebound from this blow to their career, self esteem and other hard hits in life.

After creating the company, and during product creation, I would stumble now and then on little roadblocks to product completion. Then one day, I sat down and poured out a presentation for one of the workshops that I could be proud of. So many of the ideas expressed in the presentation seemed to be ubiquitous to our culture that I wondered to myself if it was OK to include them. Then I remembered the R2A2 ideology and realized that I was on the right track.

Without thinking about it on a conscious level, I had executed the R2A2 methodology and used it successfully. Now I use it often and I encourage you to try it. Learn and internalize this simple idea as I did, and develop the habit of creating the links that help you connect the dots that can make the difference between success and failure.

W. Clement Stone says, "In order to attain any goal in life, you must first learn to Recognize, Relate, Assimilate and *Apply* principles from what you see, hear, read, think or experience."

If you really want to relate and assimilate these ideas into your own life, *work at it*. Make it a part of your implementation of the 1459 PLAN into your daily routine.

---

[8] Quantum LeapThinking; Mapes, James J.

Nine Steps that Enable Vision and Foster Achievement

Five steps for Taking an Idea from Conception, to Incubation, to Inspiration

1. Gather the raw materials. Research the immediate problem and apply information that comes from constant enrichment of your store of general knowledge.
2. Work this information over in your mind.
3. Incubate the idea in your subconscious.
4. Recognize the "Eureka! I've got it!" stage when the idea is actually born.
5. Shape and develop the idea for practical usefulness.[9]

Add this 4-Step Method to Bring Life to Ideas and for Inspiration

1. *Contemplate*—Analyze the situation
2. *Incubate*—Step back and reflect. Don't make a decision
3. *Actuate*—Consider ways to restructure the situation
4. *Integrate*—Incorporate new behavior. Gain confidence.

On a recent visit to Portugal, I was reminded to visit The Ports of the Discoveries where many years ago, men of vision set out to discover new territory, sometimes finding what they sought only after being given up as lost. Quite often, what seemed like drifting off course led to the discovery of new lands and new opportunity.

Today I think of those men when I find myself seeming to drift off course. I then use the opportunity to discover new paths to walk in life or my career and to see what new opportunity I might find there.

Develop the Habits of a Winner by Being Aware of Your:

1. Positive Self Awareness—of the abundance
2. Positive Self Esteem—of feeling good
3. Positive Self Control—of being responsible
4. Positive Self Motivation—of moving towards your dominant thoughts
5. Positive Self Expectancy—of an optimist
6. Positive Self Image—of a winner
7. Positive Self Direction—of purpose

[9] A Technique for Producing Ideas; Young, James Webb

8. Positive Self Discipline—of stimulation
9. Positive Self Dimension—of a total person
10. Positive Self Projection

Remember: You will be happy when you are doing work that has meaning to you. Work that helps propel you towards your goal.

Sew an action and you reap a habit
Sew a habit and you reap a character
Sew a character and you reap a destiny
These are the imperatives for continued success and achievement

Your inspiration to action is:

Know how—Skills/Techniques that consistently get results.
Activity Knowledge—Knowledge of the activities required
Plan and Study—Use your conscious mind to affect your subconscious mind.

To tap the powers of your subconscious you should:

➢ Use visualization and imagery
➢ Program and reprogram the unconscious idea processor
➢ Achieve alert relaxation to open the channel
➢ Use your dream power [10]

Don't put off until tomorrow the things you want to do today. Do it now, whatever it is because the sooner you start, the sooner you will finish.

The journey of hundred miles starts with one step, but you must take the initiative to begin that journey.

A true story to live by . . . .

One of my sisters—a really hard working one—was killed so horribly in an automobile accident. She died violently, in a head-on collision so severe, it tore her heart, and she died pretty much instantly. And the wind cried—Mary.

Mary had achieved pride in herself and the respect of the family by becoming a chemist for Eastman-Kodak—and yes, everyone was proud of her.

---

[10] Higher Creativity: Liberating The Unconscious For Breakthrough Insights; Harman, Willis, PhD and Rheingold, Howard

Strong ones like me are then called upon, it seems, to help with the rites. There's not just the pain of saying goodbye—there are certain rites of transition to be observed, even here.

I opened the middle drawer of her bureau and lifted out a beautiful slip—I'll never forget it. "This," I said to myself, "is not a slip. This is lingerie. This is sexy stuff." I extracted it from its little bag and handed my brother the slip. It was exquisite, fine silk, and handmade—trimmed with a wisp of lace.

The price of such a thing was certainly steep, and I bet she bought it while she was visiting somewhere special. She never wore it. She must have been saving it for a special occasion. Well, I guess this is the occasion, I mulled. Now you can wear it, girl.

My brother took the slip from me and threw it on the bed with the other clothes we were taking to the mortician. His hands were shaking, and then he slammed the door, turning to me with tears in his eyes. He said, "Don't you ever save anything for a special occasion. Every day you are alive is a special occasion!"

I remember those words. The unexpected death of the best a family has—their prodigy—has a way of drawing the best from their own black sheep. But they never knew me. We live in worlds apart, and there isn't a thing I can do about it. I thought about them on the plane returning to Chicago, my town where the family I built lives. I thought about all the things that she hadn't seen or heard or done. I thought about the things that she had done without realizing that they were special.

I'm reading more and fretting less. I'm sitting on the sill and admiring the view, my lovely lake view that I've earned, all without fussing over the things I have done or have yet to do. Those things I have yet to do are, without question, getting done. And this, that I have achieved is well earned. I'm looking forward to the next, and the next one after that.

What I draw from this experience of life lived to its fullest is this . . . it's always joy—sometimes it feels like we have a mountain to climb—the bigger the better! When we take the time to lay it out, more often than not it works in our favor.

Life is a wonderful experience, never something to be endured.

Bibliography

Hybels, Bill, *Who you are when no one's looking: Choosing consistency, resisting compromise.* InterVarsity Press, 1997

Malcolm X with Alex Haley, *The autobiography of Malcolm X*

"If I were brave" Jana Stanfield *www.JanaStanfield.com*

Believe and Achieve, Cypert, Samuel A

Success through a Positive Mental Attitude; Hill, Napoleon and Stone, W. Clement

Quantum LeapThinking; Mapes, James J.

A Technique for Producing Ideas; Young, James Webb

Higher Creativity: Liberating The Unconscious For Breakthrough Insights; Harman, Willis, PhD and Rheingold, Howard

If you have comments about this book, or would like information about other products and services offered by Yvonne Brown, contact her at:

JAD Communications International
P.O. Box 577405
Chicago, IL 60657-7405

Phone: 312-893-7527
Fax: 312-819-0423
Website: *www.JADCommunications.com*
         www.BallofGold.com
eMail: *Yvonne@jadcommunications.com*

Seminar, Keynotes and Consulting Services

International speaker, trainer, author and coach Yvonne Brown is founder of Ball of Gold Corporation and president of JAD Communications International; a firm that helps companies improve communications and relationships, manage change and expectations, improve interpersonal skills to promote respectful communications. Yvonne specifically focuses on helping people make bigger contributions, deal with conflict & difficult people and refine communications to be more productive and contribute more to the bottom line. For more information contact her at: *Yvonne@jadcommunications.com* or call 312-953-2126 today.

Visit *www.jadcommunications.com* and *www.ballofgold.com* to learn more about the author and her work.

About the Author

Yvonne F. Brown is Chief Empowerment Officer of JAD Communications®
International a motivational training and human potential firm that helps women
to be more productive and contribute more to the bottom line. She is also Founder
& President of Ball of Gold® Corporation, a knowledge management consulting
firm. With over 20 years of business management experience she has managed
major business initiatives with diverse teams within the U.S. and internationally.
She is an author who has appeared on television programs, and assists companies
with training, multi-cultural programs and digital business strategies. An
international trainer and speaker, Ms. Brown served as an adjunct professor at
the University of Illinois at Chicago for the Professional Development Program
office in the MBA department, the Business and Professional Institute at College
of DuPage & is a member of the Women's Entrepreneurship Advisory Board
at Loyola University.

Ms. Brown co-chaired the MBA/University Task Force for the Chicagoland
Entrepreneurial Center at the Chicagoland Chamber of Commerce, is Director
on the Board of the Youth Communication Organization, past President of the
Chicago Chapter of Women in Technology International (WITI), was appointed
Regional Vice President of WITI Unlimited, and is a Boardroom seminar
presenter and coach.

Ms. Brown holds a Bachelors of Arts degree in Business Management from
DePaul University and certificates in Risk Management (George Washington
University), Project Management (Loyola University) & eCommerce (University
of Illinois at Chicago). She is author of the books *Self Creation: 10 Powerful
Principles for Changing Your Life, & Proven Ways Women Overcome Obstacles
and Succeed,* and a sought after international speaker who served as a speaker
for Leadership Illinois, the University of Chicago Women's Business Group,
and the Women in Business conference for the Gannon Center for Women
and Leadership at Loyola University. Yvonne's powerful programs motivate
employees to increase efficiency, improve morale, reduce turnover, and become

more effective and productive in their work. Yvonne recently spent January of 2006 training women in the United Kingdom, and provides training programs on leadership, team building, and communications for corporations.

Active involvement in public service is evident through her participation in a variety of community organizations. Ms. Brown is a member of the National Association of Female Executives and served as the newsletter editor for the National Speaker's Association, Illinois Chapter. She was a speaker for the Gender Equity Fund of the American Association of University Women of Illinois. She has served as a member of the following committees and organizations: The IT Empowerment for Women and Girls Initiative, the Speakers Bureau for the Gender Equity Fund, the Midwest Technology Access Group a consortium which is aimed at bridging the digital divide, and the 21st Century Community Learning Center Program which is committed to Children First and improving the quality of education within the Chicago Public Schools. Ms. Brown is a member of the Advisory Board for the Women's Leadership Exchange, and a member of the Program Advisory Board of Westwood College of Technology. Ms. Brown was elected to the Steering Committee of the Chicago Minority Business Development Council (CMBDC) in 2005 and is a member of the Leadership Illinois Board of Directors.

Her leadership and commitment to excellence bring her to the forefront of organizations in which she participates. In 2002 she was inducted into the IT Professionals Hall of Fame. Ms. Brown is listed in the International Who's Who Historical Society of Professionals, the Manchester Who's Who among Executive Women, and is often quoted in technology and business magazine articles. In 2003, DePaul University selected Yvonne for inclusion in their "Alumni Success Stories-Volume II." An alumna of the Leadership Illinois Class of 2004, Ms. Brown helps people to overcome self-limiting beliefs and reach their highest potential. A candidate for the Mayor's Advisory Council on Women, Yvonne helps ordinary people produce extraordinary results.

www.JADcommunications.com—www.ballofgold.com

ORDER FORM

No	item	description	price
1	SCB001	Self Creation: 10 Powerful Principles for changing Your life	19.95
2	DFPV001	CD How to Live Your Life With Purpose and in Prosperity	24.95
3	PWB002	Proven Ways Women Overcome Obstacles and Succeed	10.00
4	SCB002	Self Creation: Workbook	15.95
5	DFPV002	Drawing Forth Your Personal Vision Workbook	15.95
6	MP3001		
7	eBook	How to write your book fast!	7.00
8	eBook	How to travel on other people's money	7.00
9	eBook	Frederick Douglas—Master Self Creator	7.00
		Subtotal	
		Shipping	
		Total	

Credit Card Information

Name as it appears on card:

Card Type: ☐ MasterCard   ☐ Visa

Card Number:

Expire Date: Month Year **Phone:**

Product Order Information

Quantity	Description	Total
		$
	Product Total	$

Customer Signature: Date: _____

We are committed to making your experience with us be the best possible for you
If you have any questions, comments, or special requests, please let us know.

BlogTalkRadio.Com/
Yvonne-F-Brown

2nd Saturday of the Month
at 2PM CST